CULTURES OF THE WORLD®

BENIN

Martha Kneib

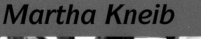

 Marshall Cavendish
Benchmark
New York

PICTURE CREDITS

Cover photo: © Sean Sprague/The Image Works

age fotostock/Kevin O'Hara: 15, 33, 51, 64, 94, 104, 112 • age fotostock/Michel Renaudeau: 44, 49, 61, 62, 107, 110 • ANA Press Agency: 6, 111, 120 • Audrius Tomonis: 135 • Bes Stock: 130 • Corbis Inc.: 9, 12, 13, 14, 18, 19, 20, 22, 31, 43, 57, 66, 68, 69,70, 72, 74, 84, 86, 88, 100, 113, 114, 116, 118, 127 • Corel Stock Photo Library: 47 • Eye Ubiquitous/Hutchison: 34, 36, 78 • Focus Team Italy: 11, 83, 93, 95, 119, 122, 125 • Getty Images: 26 • Houserstock: 56 • Lonely Planet Images: 5, 45, 50, 53, 60, 97, 109, 115 • Panos Pictures: 38, 85 • Photolibrary: 4, 54, 59, 75, 80, 108, 126 • Reuters: 1, 3, 23, 24, 27, 28, 29, 30, 77, 92, 101, 102 • Still Pictures: 90, 99, 103, 123 • Stockfood/Klaus Stemmler: 131 • Sylvia Cordaiy Photo Library: 7, 8, 81, 98, 105, 106 • Tropix.co.uk/V. and M. Birley: 37, 96, 128, 129 • Tropix.co.uk/B. McGrath: 48 • Tropix.co.uk/M. MacDonald: 124

PRECEDING PAGE

Benin supporters sing and dance before the soccer match against Morocco in the African Cup of Nations in 2004.

Marshall Cavendish Benchmark
99 White Plains Road
Tarrytown, NY 10591
Website: www.marshallcavendish.us

© Marshall Cavendish International (Asia) Private Limited 2006
® "Cultures of the World" is a registered trademark of Marshall Cavendish Corporation.

Series concept and design by Times Editions
An imprint of Marshall Cavendish International (Asia) Private Limited
A member of Times Publishing Limited

All Internet sites were correct and accurate at the time of printing.

Library of Congress Cataloging-in-Publication Data
Kneib, Martha.
  Benin / by Martha Kneib.—1st ed.
    p. cm.—(Cultures of the world)
  Summary: "Provides comprehensive information on the geography, history, governmental
    structure, economy, cultural diversity, peoples, religion, and culture of Benin"—Provided by
    publisher.
  Includes bibliographical references and index.
  ISBN-13: 978-0-7614-2328-7
  ISBN-10: 0-7614-2328-1
  1. Benin—Juvenile literature. I. Title. II. Series.
  DT541.22.K58 2006
  966.83—dc22   2005029052

Printed in China

7 6 5 4 3 2 1

CONTENTS

A Beninois with his face painted in the colors of the national flag, supports his country's soccer team during an African Cup match.

Religious rituals and ceremonies are an important part of a Beninois's life. Here a young man paints his face as part of the religious rites.

INTRODUCTION

BENIN IS A LAND of great diversity. It encompasses rain forest, savanna, and seacoast. It boasts a wealth of animals and plants and is home to many ethnic groups speaking a wide variety of languages. Benin was once the seat of several native kingdoms, but it came under the rule of the French in the 19th century. Although Benin is now independent, French is still the national language, and the French influence in the culture is still strong.

Benin, which was called Dahomey before 1975, has had a turbulent past, with many governmental changes that took place between 1960 and 1990. Benin has struggled through difficult times and economic downturns and is now working to improve its situation. With a free press and a growing economy, the country's future looks promising.

GEOGRAPHY

BENIN IS ONE of the smallest countries of Africa. It has an area of 43,488 square miles (112,633 square km). This makes it slightly smaller than the state of Pennsylvania. It is narrow from east to west, with only a 75-mile (121-km) coastline in the south. But from north to south, the country is about 430 miles (692 km) long. To the west, Benin borders Togo; to the east Nigeria; and to the north the countries Niger and Burkina Faso.

Originally much of the south was covered by rain forest, but most of this has been cleared during the centuries of human occupation. Some of it has become plantations where corn, cassava, palms, and cotton are grown. The rest has become open savanna or is lightly forested.

LANDSCAPE

There are five environmental zones within the country: the coastal area; the fertile clay area just north of the coast; the plateaus; the Atakora Mountains; and the Niger drainage plains, which are in the northeast of the country. The coastal area is unusual in that it is composed of a series of large lagoons. The only access to the sea is through outlets at Grand Popo and Cotonou.

Benin is home to national parks where one can see a range of wildlife including elephants, buffalos, hippopotamuses, crocodiles, lions, leopards, baboons, and warthogs. Pendjari National Park, which is entirely within Benin, is considered one of the most interesting game parks in West Africa. Parc National du W du Niger is shared among Benin, Burkina Faso, and Niger. It is very remote and can be accessed only by four wheel drive vehicles.

Above: **Rain forest is fast disappearing in Benin due to increased human activity and occupation.**

Opposite: **A young boy tends a herd of cows in Parakou.**

Benin's highest point is Mount Sokbaro at 2,159 feet (658 m).

7

A look at Benin's landscape. The country has a varied climate with rainy seasons, as well as dry spells and harsh winds.

CLIMATE

Benin stretches across two climatic zones. The north of the country experiences two seasons a year: a rainy season from May to September, when it receives between 37 and 48 inches (94 and 122 cm) of rain, and a dry season, when it can get as hot as 110°F (43°C) in January. Between December and March a dry wind, called the harmattan, blows from the north.

The south of the country experiences four seasons. The main rainy season runs from March to July. This is followed by a short, dry season that lasts through mid-September. A short rainy season then comes for two months, and between mid-November and March comes the main dry season. Rainfall gets heavier the farther east in the country one travels, from 32 inches (81 cm) in Grand Popo to 50 inches (127 cm) in Porto Novo. Temperatures rarely get above 95°F (35°C).

RIVERS AND LAGOONS

The Niger River constitutes the main drainage system of the country. The Niger is the third-longest river in Africa and arises in the highlands of Guinea. It passes through Mali, Niger, and Burkina Faso before crossing the border into Benin. The river drains some 1,380,000 square miles (3.57 million square km) across West Africa.

Another major river is the Pendjari, a tributary of the Volta River. It flows through Benin for 240 miles (386 km) before crossing into Togo. The Niger and the Pendjari are the major north-flowing rivers in the region.

Rivers in Benin that flow south include the Mono, the Couffo, and the Oueme. These rivers arise in the central plains of Benin and form broad floodplains in the southern coastal zone.

The sea to the south is part of the Atlantic Ocean. It is called the Bight of Benin. A bight is a wide, curving bay, and the word comes from the Old English *byht*, meaning a bend. This area used to be called the Slave Coast because the slave trade formed the basis for the economies of the local kingdoms in centuries past.

Between the coast and the Atlantic lie the coastal lagoons. The main lagoons are in Cotonou, Ouidah, Grand Popo, and Porto Novo. These lagoons are fed by the south-flowing rivers like the Oueme and are full of brackish water, which is a mix of river water and ocean water. The lagoons of Benin form just part of an extensive network of lagoons that stretches across West Africa's coast. The lagoons are separated by areas

Logs floating on the Bight of Benin.

The floodplain of the Oueme River covers more than 772 square miles (2,000 square km) at peak flood times.

of dunes and sandbars. The complex flow of tides around the many obstructions makes navigating from the coast through the lagoons and into the open ocean extremely dangerous.

The Nokoue Lagoon, which covers 12,000 acres (4,856 ha) and is, on average, only 5 feet (1.5 m) deep, was permanently connected with the Atlantic Ocean during the latter half of the 20th century. Previous to this, Nokoue Lagoon had been a major fishery in Benin, supplying much of the fish sold in the market. Yields were especially high in the 1950s. Once the lagoon was permanently connected with the ocean, however, the rise in the salt level of the water (salinity) seriously hurt the fishing industry in this area.

To combat the problem of falling fish stocks, some fishermen in Benin have turned to *acadja* fisheries to help them farm fish. In *acadja* fisheries, branches are placed upright in the water, forming a kind of corral for the fish. The preferred material for the branches is bamboo, as it lasts longer, and because algae, which some species of fish eat readily, grow on the surface of the bamboo. This means the fishermen do not have to feed the fish. Because of *acadja* enclosures, the populations of some species of fish in the lagoon are stabilizing or increasing. The most successful is a species of native tilapia called *Sarotherodon melanotheron*, which can tolerate higher salinity than other freshwater fish of the area.

Benin is a country that crosses several environmental and climatic zones, from the river valley of the Niger to the tropical lagoons of the coast. The range of climates supports a wide variety of plants, animals, and crops, including fish farms. Benin's wealth of water has helped its people farm much of the country and even supports those who make their homes on lakes. Though a tiny country in the African continent, Benin contains a great deal of geographic variety.

GANVIE, A VILLAGE ON A LAKE

One of the most unusual towns in Benin is Ganvie, which is located on a lake. Not on the lakeshore, but the lake itself! Ganvie is one of the most common places to find tourists, as it is near to Cotonou. This village is constructed of bamboo houses perched on stilts in a lagoon. The only way to get about in Ganvie is by *pirogue* (a type of canoe). Tourists can rent *pirogue*. A guide will pole the *pirogue* around the village and inform his passengers about daily life in Ganvie. Even the market of Ganvie is on the water, with women selling fish, fruits, and vegetables from their *pirogue*. Some people call Ganvie the African Venice. Approximately 15,000 people live there.

The village originated centuries ago during the era of the slave trade. The king of Dahomey was looking for more young men to sell to the Europeans for their goods. He especially wanted more guns in exchange for the slaves. Some of the Tofinu ethnic group fled to swampy areas to escape enslavement and lived off the fish and other resources of the swamp around the lake. The swamp provided food and building materials as well as protection from the Dahomean king due to a religious restriction that kept him from sending his soldiers over the water. Finally the Tofinu learned how to build their houses and live right on the lake surface itself. The name of their village breaks down to *gan* ("we are saved"), and *vie* ("community").

HISTORY

THE HISTORY OF West Africa has been shaped by many forces, one of which has been the continued spread of the Sahara desert since the end of the last Ice Age. As the desert moved south, displaced people moved ahead of it in repeated waves of immigration. These people brought new farming and metalworking techniques, and new ideas, to the area that would one day be Benin. Because these people did not appear to have brought new languages, it would seem they arrived in small groups and adopted the languages of the people around them.

Over the centuries, people became more proficient with using metal and with farming. By A.D. 1400 they were forming the first of what would later become great city-states. At this point the realm of archaeology combines with oral tradition—and a bit later, with written history—to record the kings and kingdoms that dominated Benin from this time onward.

Above: **A handpainted illustration of the Adja people of Dahomey.**

Opposite: **An illustration of villagers in one of the early kingdoms of Benin performing a ceremony with dancing and beating of drums.**

DAHOMEY

Benin was once home to one of the most famous African kingdoms, Dahomey. The oral traditions of the area tell of a people called the Adja, who migrated into the area that is now Benin during the 12th or 13th century.

The Adja founded a village called Allada. Within a few centuries this small village had grown into the center of a large state called Ardra. Ardra was ruled by kings assisted by respected elders. Around the year 1620 or 1625, three brothers had a disagreement over which one of them would be king of Ardra. One took the throne of Ardra, one founded the city that is now Porto Novo, and one founded Abomey. It was this town, Abomey, which became the center of the kingdom of Dahomey.

Wars of expansion were common in the days of the kingdom of Dahomey. In this illustration, a king leads his army into war.

Each successor of the first king, Wegbadja, pledged to leave his own successor with a bigger kingdom than he had inherited. Thus, each king was largely concerned with wars of expansion, which fueled a slave trade that made the kingdom very wealthy.

The kingdom of Dahomey was well situated for defense of its homeland. It was founded on a plateau that had more open vegetation than the tropical rain forests of the south, and it was bounded by rivers on the east and west. To the north rose steep hills and to the south was a swamp. Approaching the capital of Abomey unseen would be very difficult, and taking the kingdom by surprise with a large army would be impossible.

On the plateau itself, rainfall was generous, with the area receiving an average of 43 inches (109 cm) of rain per year. This allowed the people to grow a wide variety of crops, including millet, corn, cassava, beans, cotton, and oil palms. Thus the kings of Dahomey had a well-fed population who could contribute materials and people toward any war effort without terrible hardship.

WOMEN IN DAHOMEY

One of the unique features of the Dahomean kingdom was a dependence upon women to perform many court functions, even taking on military roles. The king was the only man permitted to live in the palace, so any court functions that took place within the palace were performed by him or by women.

A very important function was that of reign-mate, or *kpojito*. This woman never came from within the royal family but was instead a commoner. Choosing a commoner as *kpojito* may have been to symbolize the union of the king with the people of his kingdom.

The *kpojito* did not help run the kingdom, but she did perform many important ritual functions. She had her own household and retinue and was forbidden to have any contact with men other than the king. Because of this, she was a shadowy figure to the Europeans who had contacts with Dahomey, and they left no records relating the full scope of the *kpojito's* duties. However, it is known that during the 19th century, the

The king of Dahomey surrounded by women; traditionally women have played important roles in the royal court.

DAHOMEY KINGS

This is the list of names of the 11 Dahomean kings and the years they reigned. Traditionally Adonon is credited with inventing the office of *kpojito* during the reign of Agaja. Some of the dates are disputed by scholars.

Kings	Kpojito
Wegbadja (1620/25–80)	
Akaba (1680–1708)	
Agaja (1708–40)	Adonon
Tégbésu (1740–74)	Hwanjile
Kpéngla (1774–89)	Chai
Agonglo (1790–97)	Senume
Adandézan (1797–1818)	Kentobasin
Ghézo (1818–58)	Agontime
Glélé (1858–89)	Zoyindi
Béhanzin (1889–94)	Kamlin
Agoli-Agbo (1894–1900)	Kanai

Not just any son of a king was eligible to be the next king. Only those sons born after the father had been made heir to the throne could inherit the throne. Each eligible prince had to forge alliances with older, ineligible siblings, with court functionaries, and with other important men and women of the state and palace to prove his worthiness to be designated the heir over every other eligible son.

kpojito heard legal cases having to do with religious crimes and made judgments that could be appealed only to the king himself.

Another woman with influence in court was the *daklo*. She was the intermediary between the king and the people who had come to petition him or had come at his summons. No one, not even a person who had been summoned, could see the king directly. Instead the person lay on the ground on one side of a palm-leaf barrier and pled his case to the *daklo* on the other side. The *daklo* went to the king with his words and then returned to the petitioner with the king's response. Powerful men often tried to influence the *daklo*, since only she could relate their words to the king, and they wanted to make sure she would relay their words in the most flattering and positive way possible.

Royal women performed services for the king as well, including dispensing his justice. If the king wished to discipline someone, he would send out a large party of his wives to destroy or confiscate that person's property. Since touching a royal woman was a crime punishable by death, the person being disciplined could do nothing but stand aside and watch the women take or ruin his possessions.

Another function the royal women served was as spies for the king. Traditionally all women married into their husband's family in Dahomey, and their children belonged to the father. That is, with the exception of princesses. Royal women married, but neither they nor their children were part of the husband's family. Instead their loyalty was always to the king, and they would report back to the palace concerning the activities in their husband's household. By marrying princesses to powerful men, the king had access to detailed information about these men, down to what happened in their own homes.

Dahomean bards praised their king as the only man in the world with an army of women at his command.

AMAZONS

Perhaps the most interesting way in which women served the king of Dahomey was as soldiers in the army. The female soldiers of Dahomey were raised from an early age to fight hand to hand and with various kinds of weapons. They were trained to be strong and to endure suffering. Their tutors also instructed them on hunting, dancing, and playing musical instruments. Still, even though they might have some skill with music or dance, the women were not inclined toward romance or a soft life. They lived only for war. When sent into battle, they rushed into it headlong, screaming their battle cries, and fought furiously. Those who described them said they appeared to be immune to fear and pain. Neighbors of Dahomey lived in terror of them.

The French army at the port of Cotonou with Senegalese troops.

Horses in general were not used in Dahomey, because they were killed by sleeping sickness. This disease is carried by the tsetse fly.

The women warriors of Dahomey were foot soldiers. The women's main weapons were muskets, machetes, and clubs, and for the most part they did not use shields. The battle dress for the women was a half-sleeved rust-colored tunic. It was tucked in at the waist by a belt. The women also wore shorts that fell to the knees, and they fought barefoot. Around their foreheads they tied white headbands.

THE FRENCH AND THE END OF DAHOMEY

The kingdom of Dahomey expanded rapidly. In 1724 it captured the neighboring kingdom of Allada, and in 1727 it captured another kingdom, Ouidah. Capturing Ouidah, a coastal city, gave Dahomey access to the sea. This also gave Dahomey access to trade with the Europeans, especially the French. However, the Yoruba kingdom of Oyo, which was situated to the east of Dahomey, was strong enough to conquer Dahomey in 1730. It was not until 1818, under King Ghézo, that Dahomey regained its independence. During the 1800s the kingdom was at its largest and most powerful, but by 1900 the French had deposed the last Dahomean king. Dahomey was under European rule.

After the French had moved into the area and effectively conquered the local kingdoms, they began their colonial rule. Missionaries established missions, and schools were set up. Most of these activities took place in the south of the country, with fewer missionaries and educators being found the farther one got from the coast. The French also tried to increase the agricultural potential of the country. As for mineral resources, they were few and located inland, which made them hard to exploit.

Hubert Maga (*left*) and other African leaders at the Elysee Palace in France.

INDEPENDENCE

Independence from France came on August 1, 1960. At that time the country had a weak economy and a population splintered into many ethnic and regional divisions. Factions within the major political party of the time, the Union Progressiste Dahomeenne, kept the nation destabilized with conflicts and power plays among members. Within a short time, three main political groups under strong leaders were formed. One was in the southeast under Sourou Migan Apithy, a leader from the Yoruba. Another was centered around Justin Ahomadegbe, a descendent of a royal family, in the Fon and Adja areas in the center and southwest of the country. The third was in the north under Hubert Maga, a former school teacher turned politician who could count on the Bariba vote.

A military tank patrols the streets of Dahomey after the government collapsed in 1965.

None of these three groups could gain the upper hand for long. The 1960s were full of political infighting, student strikes, and strikes by trade unions. The first major collapse occurred on October 29, 1963. Benin's government had been championing austerity policies designed to make the country more fiscally stable. At the same time, however, the government was full of corruption and spent large amounts of money on luxuries. This led to massive demonstrations. A new government was formed in January 1964, but it collapsed in September 1965. Another new government was created with Tahirou Congacou, president of the National Assembly, in charge. However, Congacou was not able to work with others well enough to form a stable government, and three months later Christophe Soglo, an army officer, assumed control of the country.

In 1967 a group of junior army officers ousted Soglo and replaced him with Major Maurice Kouandete. According to popular belief, Soglo learned he had been ousted when someone knocked on his door and said, "You're through." Indeed, no regime leader was killed during any of Benin's numerous coups.

Kouandete, like his predecessors, could not get political rivals to stop fighting long enough to form a stable government, and his administration also failed quickly.

A presidential election was to be held in 1968 in an attempt to resolve the situation, but old leaders such as Apithy called for a boycott of the election, and 83 percent of the electorate stayed home. In the wake of this disaster, another military regime, this one under Emile Zinsou, was formed, but it lasted only until December 10, 1969. Zinsou was at a particular disadvantage because he was "Brazilian," that is, his ancestors had returned to Benin from the Americas, where they had been slaves. Thus he had no direct ethnic ties to any community.

Zinsou was soon removed from power by Kouandete, but the officer corps of the army refused to recognize him as the leader of the country. Instead the army proposed a military directorate that would be led by several men; however, these men also could not put aside their differences. Elections were held, with the situation after the elections resembling the situation of a decade before, with Apithy, Ahomadegbe, and Maga winning the vote in the southeast, the southwest and central, and the north, respectively.

The directorate suspended the results of the elections, and in consequence each section of Benin threatened to secede from the others. Finally Maga, Apithy, and Ahomadegbe agreed to serve as "co-presidents." Their term was marked, like those of their predecessors, by fiscal mismanagement and corruption.

The name "Benin" was taken from the Nigerian kingdom of Benin.

Mathieu Kerekou (*center*), former president of the People's Republic of Benin, as the country was then called, on an official visit to China in 1977.

THE BENINOIS REVOLUTION

On October 26, 1972, the army launched its sixth coup d'état. Although at the time it did not seem much different from the other five, this one would change Benin forever. This particular coup was orchestrated by officers from the Ouidah garrison, who recruited Major Mathieu Kerekou to lead the new regime. Anyone connected to the former government was retired or placed under arrest in military camps away from their bases of power.

During the 1970s Kerekou moved the country toward a socialist government, one in which the state was in control of nearly every business and economic activity. Consequently foreign investment in the country—never very sizeable to begin with—disappeared. The country, up until then called Dahomey, was renamed the People's Republic of Benin. The army and the political system were reorganized to reflect the new political climate. A new constitution endorsed the new political organization and decreed a joining of civil and military authority positions.

The new regime under Kerekou was called the Beninois Revolution. During the 1970s, however, the revolutionary Beninois government failed to live up to its ideology. What little natural resources the country had were squandered, and the economy was in turmoil. Some areas did see progress, as roads and tourist facilities reached into the northern half of the country where they never had before. Cotton production, too, began to rise. But Benin's problems were too large to be offset much by these small gains.

Reorganization of the educational system resulted in a mass exodus of trained teachers from the country. Other professionals also left the country in great numbers. As a result, despite a high birth rate, the overall

Former president Kerekou (*left*) in a meeting with French president, Jacques Chirac. France is an important economic and cultural partner of Benin.

Nicephore Soglo won Benin's democratic presidential elections in 1991.

population of the country did not increase. The lack of trained people in a number of professions severely hampered industry and education.

The difficulty the ruling military regime had in controlling the country spilled over into the regime itself. Cabinet meetings erupted into fistfights. Ministers argued with each other endlessly. Key areas of government were practically frozen, unable to perform their functions.

By 1981, 92 percent of the country's budget had been designated as payroll for bureaucrats. The need for income resulted in Benin signing an agreement with France to take its nuclear waste for only 10 percent of what other nations charged. Money from offshore oil wells helped, but it was not enough. In 1989 mass demonstrations against the government spurred a governmental collapse. Riots broke out, and there was no money to pay or supply the army. The banking system collapsed. The nuclear-waste contracts were canceled after it came to light that Kerekou planned to bury the waste near Abomey, a move the southerners felt was designed by a northern ruler to eliminate them.

DEMOCRACY

Kerekou had to accept that his socialist revolution had failed and the country was in desperate straits. His own aide, the Archbishop of Cotonou, and France urged Kerekou to assemble a national convention to discuss how to solve the nation's problems. He did, and a nine-day convention was held. Even ex-regime leaders and Beninois living abroad attended.

Kerekou's 18-year reign was criticized by everyone, and Kerekou, with no way to pay for continued military rule, was forced to accept the convention's advice. A new constitution would be drawn up and ratified on December 10, 1990. Political prisoners were released, and socialism was abandoned. Benin would become a democracy, and multiparty elections would be held in 1991.

By the time of the elections, 34 political parties had been organized, and 1,400 people were running for 65 seats in the National Assembly. Fourteen men ran for president, but the only serious contenders for the job were Nicephore Soglo and Kerekou. Each won his own area of the country: Soglo the south and Kerekou the north. Soglo was elected president, and his party won most of the seats in the National Assembly.

Kerekou ran successfully for the presidency in 1996, ousting Soglo, who won the seat of mayor of Cotonou in February 2002. In 2006 Yayi Boni won the presidential election, defeating Adrien Houngbédji with 75 percent of the vote. Though still very poor and facing complicated problems, Benin has found a new confidence in its place in the world. The country has strengthened its ties with France and the United States, has acted as mediator in crises elsewhere in the world such as in Liberia and Togo, and has sent soldiers to serve in the United Nations force in Haiti.

Benin has a rich and storied history and was home to one of the most celebrated kingdoms of Africa, a kingdom that was one of the only regimes ever to use entire units of women warriors. The country stumbled for many years after independence, ousting first one dictator, then another, and experimented with socialism, but in the end the country was bankrupt and the army grew beyond the president's control. Democracy was implemented in 1990, and since then Benin has made some strides toward resolving its debt and regaining its rightful place among its neighbors and the world.

GOVERNMENT

BENIN HAS A MULTIPARTY democracy currently headed by Yayi Boni. The people are represented by their elected officials, who meet in the National Assembly and who make the laws, and by the president, who is responsible for the day-to-day running of the country. To ensure that laws are followed, the country has a Supreme Court, similar to that of the United States. Benin has struggled in the past with problems such as favoritism and corruption, which have kept Benin from progressing as rapidly as it could have. But the democracy is still young, and there is no sign that it is failing, so in the future perhaps Benin will be able to overcome many of the problems of its past.

Above: **An enthusiastic crowd welcomes Yayi Boni (*right*) with flags and cheers after he is elected president of Benin.**

Opposite: **A billboard on the streets of Cotonou supports Yayi Boni's campaign to be elected president in 2006.**

THE GOVERNMENT

The government in Benin is headed by a president, who is elected by the people to a five-year term. Voting is universal for people 18 and over. The president appoints his cabinet. In the elections of March 22, 2001, Mathieu Kerekou was reelected president with 84.1 percent of the vote. His opponent, Bruno Amoussou, received 15.9 percent of the vote.

In March 2006 presidential elections were held once again. Kerekou was not eligible to run for the presidency due to a two-term limit and an age cut-off. His opponent in the 1991 election, Nicephore Soglo, was also ineligible because of his age. An astounding 81 percent of the electorate came to the polls on March 5; however, since no single candidate won over 50 percent of the votes, a run-off election had to be held on March 19.

Benin's national anthem is "L'aube Nouvelle," ("The New Dawn").

Yayi Boni was elected president after getting 75 percent of the votes in the presidential elections of March 2006.

In the run-off Yayi Boni won the presidential election by garnering almost 75 percent of the votes. Voter turnout was estimated to have been 67 percent of the electorate.

Boni has worked for the West African Development Bank (BOAD) since 1994 and has had no previous experience in politics. Some feel this outsider status made him more popular with the voters. His family is from the north of Benin. He was educated in the field of economics; therefore, it was no surprise that the main focus of his election campaign was economic reform. Boni took office on April 6, 2006.

The National Assembly consists of 83 members who are elected by direct popular vote to four-year terms. Elections were last held on March 30, 2003, and will be held again in March 2007.

Many political parties are active in Benin. Some of them are the Presidential Movement, which holds 52 seats in the National Assembly; the Renaissance Party du Benin (PRB); the Democratic Renewal Party

MATHIEU KEREKOU

The former president of Benin was born on September 2, 1933, in the town of Kouarfa, which is in the north of the country. He studied at schools in the countries of Mali and Senegal and then joined the French army. He furthered his schooling while in the army at a training college in Paris.

In the early 1960s Kerekou was the aide of then-president Hubert Maga. He took power in 1972 and pursued a socialist agenda until 1990. In 1991, when the first multiparty elections were held, Kerekou lost the presidency, but he was elected president in 1996 and again in 2001.

(PRD); and Alliance E'toile (Star Alliance). These four parties hold the bulk of the National Assembly seats.

The judicial system of Benin consists of a Constitutional Court, a Supreme Court, and a High Court of Justice. The laws of Benin generally follow French civil law. Traditional laws are also recognized.

THE PRESIDENT

In Benin the president of the republic serves as the head of state. He is responsible for guaranteeing national independence, territorial integrity, and respect for the constitution, treaties, and other international agreements. He is elected to a five-year term and may serve a maximum of two terms.

To be eligible to run for presidency, a person must be Beninois by birth or a citizen for at least 10 years. He must be at least 40 but no more than 70 years old, live in Benin, and must be considered healthy, both physically and mentally, by a committee of three doctors appointed by a constitutional court.

THE CIVIL CABINET

The civil cabinet is the organization responsible for advising the president. The president puts forward the names of the people he wishes to be on the cabinet, and the Council of Ministers approves them. Members of the civil cabinet include a cabinet director, a deputy cabinet director, a principal private secretary, a protocol manager, and others such as technical advisers. The cabinet director coordinates the activities of this body.

People in Benin vote by placing their fingerprint next to the name or picture of the candidate they support. Here, a woman casts her vote at a presidential election.

The cabinet is responsible for designing strategies for the president, providing advice and information on both national and international situations and issues, and ensuring the development and follow-through of programs and policies designed by the president.

THE NATIONAL ASSEMBLY

This group is chaired by a president of the assembly, elected by the members from their own ranks, and assisted by a board. Members are called MPs (members of parliament). Each MP is elected to a term of four years and may be reelected. MPs do not represent a particular area of the country; each one represents the country as a whole.

The National Assembly meets for two sessions each year. The first session starts in the first half of April, and the second begins in the first half of October. These sessions cannot be any longer than three months. If the president wishes, he can call an emergency session during those times of the year when the National Assembly is not already meeting. These emergency sessions cannot be any longer than 15 days.

THE CONSTITUTIONAL AND SUPREME COURTS

The Constitutional Court of Benin is composed of seven people. Three of them are judges with a minimum of 15 years experience. Two of the members of the court are professors or practitioners of the law, with a minimum of 15 years experience. The two remaining members must be people of good professional reputation. The National Assembly appoints four of these judges, and the president of the republic appoints the other three.

These seven judges cannot be removed from office. Unless they commit a serious crime, they cannot be arrested or sued. Members of the Constitutional Court are not allowed to hold any other occupation, including civil or military employment, while they are serving on the court. Part of the responsibilities of this court is to ensure the lawfulness of ballots and the results of elections.

Above: **As its economic and political situation improves, Benin is increasing its presence on the world stage. Here, Queen Elizabeth II greets Beninois Ambassador Edgar-Yves Monnou.**

Opposite: **The Beninois have started playing a more active role in politics since the establishment of multiparty democracy.**

The Supreme Court is the highest court in the land. There are seven members of the court. Once the Supreme Court has made a decision in a case, there can be no appeals.

The Supreme Court is responsible for restraining the president and the National Assembly from abusing their powers; for overseeing decisions rendered by lower courts; for controlling the accounts of the election campaigns; and for providing advice on the legality of bills before they are sent to the National Assembly.

DIVIDING THE COUNTRY

The French had divided the country into six *départements*, which were administrative units similar to the states in the United States. The six *départements* were Atakora, Atlantique, Borgou, Mono, Oueme, and Zou. These were subdivided into 35 *sous-préfectures* and further subdivided into 75 *arrondissements*.

In 1974 the *départements* were renamed provinces, and the *sous-préfectures* were renamed districts. The six provinces retained their old

TOURISM

Benin's government is composed of many ministries. One of these is the Ministry of Culture, Craft Industry, and Tourism (MCAT). This ministry is responsible for promoting the country and its tourist trade and for providing information and technical assistance to those in the tourism industry.

In the past MCAT has been active in promoting Benin by aiding its participation in such international events as the Holidays Exhibition in Brussels; the World Tourism Organization in Beijing; the African Arts Gallery in Abidjan, Ivory Coast; and the Pan-African Movie and Television Festival of Ouagadougou, Burkina Faso.

A day in a village in Oueme, one of the 12 provinces of Benin.

boundaries but were subdivided into 84 districts and subdivided again into 404 communes. Advisory councils were set up at the district and province levels. These councils were given the power to make decisions on local matters, policymaking, and finance. However, this scheme broke down and was gone by the mid-1990s.

On January 15, 1999, the country's six provinces were divided into 12 departments: Alibori, Atakora, Atlantique, Borgou, Collines, Donga, Kouffo, Littoral, Mono, Oueme, Plateau, and Zou. Some of these departments do not have administrative capitals yet.

Benin's government has changed a great deal since the days when military officers replaced one another in repeated coups. Today the government is elected by the people, and there are courts, a National Assembly, and a cabinet to oversee legal cases, to pass laws, and advise the president. Future elections are already scheduled, and Benin's fledgling democracy appears to be functioning well.

ECONOMY

ECONOMIC GROWTH in Benin has been slow in coming. An open-market economy was only adopted in 1990, so the country is still trying to create many infrastructures and industries from scratch. Still, growth has been remarkable during the past 15 years, and with much of Benin's foreign debt eased, growth should continue into the foreseeable future.

The change to a free-market system in 1990 has helped Benin regain some stability and growth in its economy. Private businesses and investments are growing, and several laws have been passed which are designed to make Benin more attractive to foreign investors.

Until the 1970s much of what was exported from the country came from the palm plantations. However, the profits from palm products had never been enough to fuel a great deal of economic growth, employment opportunities, and social services. After the 1970s, exports of cotton and the production of oil from offshore oil fields increased the country's wealth. The oil fields have since ceased production, and today the main base of Benin's economy is agriculture.

AGRICULTURE

Traditionally, Benin's economy has depended upon agriculture, and agriculture remains the single most important sector of Benin's economy. The "king of crops" is cotton, most of which is grown in the district of Borgou. Today, Benin is the leading cotton producer in West Africa.

In 1993 alone, cotton accounted for 89 percent of Benin's export earnings. Because of this dependence upon a single crop, Benin's economy is unfortunately easily affected by the world market prices for cotton.

Cotton is the main source of income for Benin's farmers, accounting for nearly 75 percent of household income. Only 3 percent of household income is gained through raising food crops. Because the economy, as

Opposite: **The busy port of Cotonou has surpassed the port of Lagos in Nigeria in cargo traffic.**

Agriculture employs 85 percent of Benin's population.

well as farmers' household income, is so dependent upon cotton, production increases every year as farmers attempt to increase their profits. In 1982, 30,400 tons of seed cotton was planted. By 1994 that figure was 273,000 tons. During the same period, the land under cotton cultivation rose from 65,483 acres (26,500 ha) to 504,566 acres (205,000 ha).

In the long term, cotton production in Benin is threatened by environmental degradation and pollution. Also, Benin lacks the ginning facilities to handle a constantly-expanding cotton harvest. The government sets quotas on seeds in certain ecological zones, but the farmers in those areas have found other ways to obtain the seeds and the government's attempt to limit production has failed.

A field of harvested cotton; cotton is Benin's main export.

Depleting the soil by not rotating crops, soil erosion, the use of pesticides, and the continual clearance of forests are other ways in which cotton production threatens to damage the ecology of Benin. Although the farmers and the government are aware of these issues, satisfactory solutions to the problems of cotton production have not yet been agreed upon or implemented.

One proposed solution is to exploit a growing market for organically grown cotton fibers, which could be sold at a higher price than the rest of the cotton harvest. The increased price which could be demanded for organic cotton would help offset the increased cost in farming without further damaging the environment. However, worries about the long-term viability of the organic cotton market have kept this proposal from being implemented at this time.

INDUSTRY

Benin has very little industry, though in the future, with more reliable access to electricity and natural gas, industries are likely to move into the country and be successful.

The country has one cement plant, which is located in Onigbolo. This plant produces 2,039,275,923 pounds (925,000 metric tons) of cement per year. Benin also has a sugar refinery in Savé. The West African Development Bank assisted in revitalizing a textile factory in Parakou. Other industries include two shrimp-processing plants, a soft-drink plant, a brewery, and several cotton ginning facilities. Palm oil processing plants are located in Ahozon, Avrankou, Bohicon, Cotonou, Gbada, and Pobe.

Over two-thirds of Benin's exports go to Niger and Nigeria. Unfortunately, smuggling across the Nigerian border has prompted Nigeria to tighten its border controls. One of the main products smuggled over the border is gasoline. Smuggled gas is known as *kpayo* and is sold at roadside stands by people who have often been in the smuggling trade for 20 years or more. Although the quality of the *kpayo* is not always good, it is cheaper than the gasoline at the pump.

Beninois authorities have rarely attempted to halt or control the trade in *kpayo*; a rare crackdown in Porto Novo by authorities in August 2004 killed four people. However, the crackdown brought about riots by locals.

Other products such as textiles and food are also smuggled across the border. Cars stolen in Nigeria often turn up for sale in Benin. The problem is so widespread, that in 2003, Nigeria closed its border with Benin to protest the rampant smuggling and the lack of response by the Beninois

Smuggled gasoline from Nigeria on sale at a roadside stall in Benin.

government. Another reason for the border closure may have had been Nigeria's concern that the port of Lagos in Nigeria had lost business to Cotonou in Benin. Cargo traffic is handled more efficiently in Cotonou, which means the owners of the goods can get their wares unloaded in Cotonou and shipped by truck to Nigeria more quickly and cheaply than taking the goods directly to Lagos. However, this means huge losses in port and customs revenues for Nigeria.

Human trafficking is also a problem in Benin: children destined for forced labor and prostitution are smuggled out of Benin and into Nigeria, Ghana, Gabon, Cote d'Ivoire, and Cameroon. Others from Niger, Togo, and Burkina Faso are brought into Benin for domestic labor. Many of these children end up working in rock quarries and cocoa plantations. Though the government of Benin has made some attempts to put a stop to this, it has not yet been able to cause any significant decrease in human trafficking across Benin's borders.

Immediately after taking office as president on April 6, 2006, Yayi Boni traveled to Nigeria and visited Nigeria's president, Olusegun Obasanjo, to discuss border difficulties. The two called for enhanced security at border posts and for increased cooperation between Nigerian and Beninois officials in order to rein in smuggling. Obasanjo ordered 10 new vehicles fitted with communications equipment to be added to joint border patrols. He also proposed a joint commission between the two countries which would meet biannually to review the countries' progress in the strengthening of their relations.

Yayi Boni said that he had made Nigeria his first official visit after his inauguration because of the importance of Benin's relationship with Nigeria. Perhaps, in the future, the border between Nigeria and Benin will see more legal than illegal trade.

The average salary for an agricultural worker is 80 CFA/hour ($0.15/hour).

MINERALS

An estimated 500 million metric tons of iron ore has been identified in Loumbou-Loumbou in the Borgou district. No attempt has been made to develop this resource at this time.

Benin has several exploitable natural resources, including gold, iron ore, phosphates, and petroleum.

Gold is found in the Atakora Mountains in the northwestern part of the country, along the Perma River. Mining began during the colonial era; the government of Benin itself took up gold mining in the mid-1960s. However, the effort was abandoned in the mid-1980s. After that, individuals from northern Benin, joined by migrant miners from the countries of Burkina Faso and Togo, began to mine for gold in the area.

The land is still held by the government of Benin, and in 1996, the government used militia to confiscate the mining equipment and personal property of the miners in an effort to halt their unregulated activities. The miners refused to be run off, and eventually the government accepted their presence and officially began to allow small-scale mining.

In 1982 Benin began producing petroleum from two wells from the Semé oil field. Average production began around 8,000 barrels a day, but this amount dwindled over time to approximately 1,900 barrels a day. In 1998 the oil field was shut down. A South African company, Industrial Development Corporation Ltd., has expressed an interest in reopening the oil field, but so far this has not happened.

Deposits of phosphates have been identified in both northern and southern areas of the country. So far, exploitation of these resources has been determined to be uneconomical and they remain undeveloped.

One of the reasons that such resources remain undeveloped is that they are in remote, inaccessible areas. Recent improvements in infrastructure, such as the Djougou-Ndali interstate national road project, which connects Benin with Nigeria and Togo, may eventually change this.

ELECTRICITY AND FUEL

Few people in Benin have access to reliable electricity, and the demand for it rises every year. In the north of the country, especially, people are used to frequent disruptions in their service. These brownouts not only interrupts people's lives, but slows economic development.

Much of the country's electricity is imported from Ghana. However, two dams on the Mono River, the Nangbeto Dam and the Adjarala Dam, are expected to provide much of the country's electricity when both become operational. These projects were accomplished in partnership with the government of Togo. Although the dams will help ease the country's power problems, the construction of the dams has displaced thousands of people in both Benin and Togo.

SOLAR POWER

The Solar Electric Light Fund (SELF) is working on a plan to provide electricity produced by solar power to 44 villages in Borgou. Currently, 95 percent of the people in these villages are farmers, and many of them depend entirely on rain to irrigate their crops. Their ability to grow enough to feed their families is often limited in times of drought and growing surplus food is often not possible.

Other sources of water are wells or streams, but this water must be drawn and transported by hand. A few people may have water pumps that are run by gas-powered motors, but these are very expensive to acquire, and impossible to repair and maintain for long.

Solar-powered pumps will help farmers by drawing water from wells and sending it through irrigation canals to the fields all year round. Dependence on rainfall will be diminished. With greater access to water, farmers will be able to grow crops more reliably and will also be able to grow crops during dry seasons. They should not only be able to feed their families, but ought to be able to grow surplus food to sell.

Local people will also be trained to install and maintain the equipment; thus, the pumps should be sustainable over the long run. If this project is successful, it will be expanded to other districts.

Benin has also participated in the plan to build the West African Gas Pipeline (WAGS), a 620-mile (1,033-km) natural gas pipeline which runs from Nigeria to Ghana. A study commissioned by the oil company Chevron estimates that up to 60,000 jobs will be created in the four countries where the pipeline is located (Nigeria, Benin, Togo, Ghana) when new industry is attracted to the area. The World Bank estimates that the countries will save $500 million in energy costs over the next 20 years by using natural gas in place of more expensive fuels. However, along with increased industry and cheaper power, the plan may ultimately displace up to 50,000 families across West Africa.

DEBT RELIEF

In 2003 the International Money Fund (IMF) and the World Bank's International Development Association (IDA) agreed that Benin had met the requirements for $460 million in debt relief over time. Benin was the eighth country to achieve the requirements set by the international organizations. The plan would decrease Benin's debt by nearly 31 percent. The IMF and IDA noted that Benin's economy had maintained a steady 5 percent growth rate since 1990, but also that the country was heavily dependent upon the price of cotton. Since cotton forms the bulk of Benin's exports, a drop in cotton prices would be ruinous. The immediate effect of the plan was that Benin spent 54 percent of its savings on health care.

Benin's debt woes were further reduced in 2005. Eighteen nations, including Benin, were named by the Group of Eight (G8) countries as those who are to have a significant portion of their debts cleared. G8 finance ministers said that countries who had met minimum standards of good governance could have their debts forgiven if they would use

the money that would have gone toward debt payment for health care, hospital construction, education, and toward the salaries of nurses and teachers. The Benin Minister of State for Planning and Development called the agreement "a historic decision."

Benin is due to have a debt of more than $800 million dollars eliminated. The debt is owed by the country to the World Bank, the International Money Fund, and the African Development Bank, and represents 63 percent of the country's foreign debt. Previous debt relief to Benin had resulted in the country allocating more funds to health and education. Primary school fees, especially for girls, were subsidized by the government with $5.6 million. By using the money in this way, Benin hopes to meet its obligations under an agreement by world leaders at the United Nations Millennium Summit in 2000 that developing countries should achieve universal primary education of their children by 2015.

Benin's economy is dependent on the export of cotton; a drop in the demand or price of cotton will have a heavy impact on the country.

ENVIRONMENT

BENIN IS A LAND rich in wildlife. The effect of rising human population on the animals and plants of the region have been severe, however. For instance, across West Africa more than 90 percent of the rain forest has been cut down. The plants and animals that live in the forests have been pushed into small, isolated pockets of forest that are still under threat from logging companies and even from the locals, who need firewood and meat to feed their families. Fortunately many programs have been established to help alleviate the problems.

ENDANGERED FORESTS

In the south of the country, the mangrove forests have been largely deforested. People need the wood for use in their cooking fires. To help alleviate the pressure on the mangrove forests, tree plantations are being established. The seedlings grow quickly into trees and are available for women to use as firewood. Also, seedlings are planted in the remainder of the mangrove forests in order to rejuvenate the area. This project is still under way.

The Niaouli and Lokoli forests are threatened by timber companies that pay the local villagers for the right to cut down the trees in their areas. These forests are home to several endangered species, including the red-bellied guenon and another monkey, Geoffroy's Pied Colobus. Many rare birds either live in these rain forests or stop there on their migrations. Protective measures such as guards and education for local villagers, as well as reforesting some areas, have resulted in the return of a few species to the forests.

Above: **Deforestation threatens forests like this one at Boukoumba, near Natitingou.**

Opposite: **Coconut groves are a common sight on Benin's coast, which is relatively unspoiled by human activity.**

45

ENDANGERED ANIMALS

*A single West
African manatee
is on display at the
Toba Aquarium
in Japan.*

The West African manatee is now considered endangered. Manatees are mammals that look something like walruses; their forelimbs are flippers, and their hind limbs form a broad, flat paddle. The West African manatee has been the least studied of all manatee species. It lives in rivers, estuaries, and shallow coastal waters. Because this species is not well known, there are few pictures of it, and scientists know little about it but assume it to be very similar to other manatee species.

Crocodiles and sharks occasionally kill manatees, but the main threat to them is from humans, by poaching or through habitat destruction. Pollution is also a threat to the manatees, as are fishing nets: manatees need to surface to breathe air, so they will drown if caught in fishing nets. Because some manatees feed largely on mangroves, the loss of the mangrove forests is a direct threat to their survival. It is illegal in Benin to capture or kill manatees, but their population is still in decline, mostly due to loss of habitat. The organization Nature Tropicale is working to find ways to save the manatees and their habitat.

Other animals under threat in Benin include sea turtles, hippopotamuses, and crocodiles. The crocodiles have been threatened by cotton production, because the runoff of pesticides from the cotton fields has poisoned them. Also, much of the water where they live has been pumped away to irrigate cotton fields. The threat to the sea turtles is so great that in 2000, Benin, the Netherlands, and Costa Rica held an exchange program to research the turtles and find ways to protect them. People from many West African nations participated. Egg nurseries have been developed to help ensure that enough turtle eggs hatch and the young turtles make it to the ocean. Also, local villagers were educated about the importance of saving turtles and their habitat.

Another species under pressure in Benin, the red-bellied guenon, is a tree-dwelling monkey that usually weighs between 4.4 pounds and 9.9 pounds (2 kg and 4.5 kg). It lives in tropical areas and prefers the wettest parts of the forest. It eats fruit, insects, and leaves. Guenons usually live in small groups of five to 30 individuals. In 2000 the status of this species changed from "vulnerable" to "endangered," due to a continued decline in the population because of hunting and loss of habitat. This particular species is found only in southwestern Nigeria and southern Benin, so it is very important that it is protected. An international action plan is being devised to help maintain the guenon's habitat and keep its numbers from dwindling further.

A pilot project designed to help the red-bellied guenons was developed in the village of Togbota. Villagers were very interested in finding ways to assist the survival of the monkeys and agreed to be involved with a Dutch TV show that documented the monkeys' plight.

Measures taken to educate people regarding the protection of sea turtles have helped the species to survive.

The wildlife of Benin is a draw for ecotourists around the world.

ECOTOURISM

Many of Benin's conservation goals can be met if more money is generated by ecotourism. Ecotourists are those who travel to an area to observe wildlife and learn about the environment, often under the guidance of local experts or university staff. Those who travel with ecotourism in mind often try to learn whatever they can to spread information back home about what can be done to help the environmental problems they have seen close up. In Benin plans to promote tourism at places like the Niaouli forest will help educate people about Benin's problems, inform them of what can be done, and bring money into the area at the same time. The sea turtle egg nurseries may also attract ecotourists.

One area where Benin may have luck in attracting ecotourism is with whale- and dolphin-watching ventures. Scientists have discovered that humpback whales do swim in Beninois waters during certain times of the year and that the dolphin population is very high year-round. Two

AGROTOURISM

A new form of tourism that may benefit Benin's people is agrotourism. This is when tourists are allowed to view the agricultural methods in planting, growing, harvesting, and processing relating to the crops grown in the region. Since many of the crops and the products made from them are not found in most tourists' home countries, they may find the tours very interesting as well as informative. One advantage of agrotourism programs is that they generally benefit the local farmers more than other sorts of tourism programs.

boats have already been converted for tourism purposes, and the long-term ability of the country to sustain ecotourism seems assured.

Many of Benin's animals and plants are under threat of extinction due to loss of habitat, poaching, and pesticides. Because most of the people of Benin are very poor, it is very important not only to educate them on which animals and plants need protecting but also to give them the tools they need to survive so that they do not further harm their local environment out of necessity. Most people have been eager to help once approached. In the future, it may be possible for the Beninois and their visitors to appreciate the many wonderful animals and plants of the country.

BENINOIS

ROUGHLY 42 ETHNIC GROUPS live in Benin. Several of the larger groups are the Bariba in the north, the Yoruba in the southeast, and the Fon in the south and central areas of the country. These people often live side by side, and their children may grow up learning several languages in addition to their own and the national language, French. Benin is a quilt of many customs and traditions, which make it a rich and interesting place to study or visit.

THE BARIBA

The Bariba live in central and northern Benin and are largely Muslim. They make up about 8.5 percent of Benin's population. During the 19th century the Bariba lived in independent kingdoms such as Nikki and Kandi.

Above: **In Benin, the large number of ethnic groups, customs, and traditions make up a culturally diverse society.**

Opposite: **The happy face of a young girl with her mother. There are many traditional beliefs and rituals associated with childhood among the various ethnic groups in Benin.**

The Bariba count their descent from a legendary ancestor called Kisira. Kisira was an Arabic warrior from the seventh century A.D. who refused to convert to Islam. He left his home an exile and traveled across Africa to found the original Bariba state at Borgou. Later, this state split into several smaller states, including Nikki, which is the dominant Bariba state in Benin. By the time of the French colonization, the Nikki dynasty had given rise to 28 kings.

After the French occupation, Nikki lost power due to its position on the extreme northern end of the colony, away from most of the trade routes. Today, Nikki is a small town which is connected to Benin's main north-south highway by a dirt road. Although the traditional reverence connected to Nikki has faded over time, the town is still significant enough that all political candidates from the north make a point to pay their ritual respects to the king of the Bariba who resides in Nikki.

A Bariba proverb states, "Between death and shame, death has the greater beauty."

Among the Bariba, one of the most important attributes parents want to instill in their children is stoic behavior in the face of pain or grief. For instance, the ideal woman is one who gives birth at home, without assistance and without anyone knowing she was ever in labor. Only when the baby is born and the woman calls out for someone to help her cut the cord and clean up the child should anyone else know what is going on.

When medical clinics were opened in the north of the country, the non-Bariba staff were amazed at the stoic endurance of their patients. In the south such silent endurance of pain is not prized as highly as it is among the Bariba.

NAMING A BARIBA CHILD

Newborn children are immediately given a name that represents their place in the family, for instance first daughter or third son, and they may be given a Muslim name when they are 8 days old. But it is not until the child is 4 or 5 years old that he or she receives his or her own name. Children lack the ability to reason, and so their entry into Bariba society follows a progression rather than happening all at once at birth.

CIRCUMCISION

In the past male and female Bariba children were routinely circumcised. This practice, at least for girls, is now illegal in Benin. It is still carried out, however, mostly in rural areas. It is difficult to know how widespread the practice is, since those who still follow it are doing so illegally. Many Bariba consider girls who have not been circumcised to live in *sekuru*, a state of shame, so there is great social pressure on girls and their families to conform to the old custom.

WITCHES AMONG THE BARIBA

Despite their conversion to Islam, the Bariba believe in sorcery. They will protect their children from evil spells by using amulets, such as strings or waistbands, or folk medicines. The Bariba keep a wary eye out for several kinds of magic and folk illnesses. One of the things they are most concerned about is the presence of witch children among them.

Babies born as witches are referred to as *biiyondo*. The Bariba believe that witches are simply born witches and cannot help what they are. Their very presence will cause bad things to happen to the people around them due to their inborn evil power. Babies who are born witches may be discovered by such signs as breech

A Beninois mother and child. Many Beninois women fear giving birth to "witch babies."

birth, being born with teeth, having their teeth first erupt in the upper jaw, being born too early, and with birth defects. In the past children who were believed to be born witches were killed by a local specialist or through parental neglect.

When modern clinics were first established in the Bariba area, many women refused to give birth there because they would not have the same control over the disposition of the infant that they would at home. In the clinics, the women could not be assured that the medical staff would recognize the signs of a witch birth or would do what was necessary to dispose of the witch. Women feared being sent home with a witch child.

Although laws were passed making home births illegal, many women preferred to pay the fine and give birth at home. But as clinic births become more common, new rituals have been conceived that promise to neutralize the witch baby's power without killing the child. The neutralization

Maternity clinics are becoming more common and accepted in the more developed parts of Benin.

requires herbs and fumigation, but many people do not have any faith that such spells will work. Therefore, such babies are still in danger of being abandoned or killed. Sometimes, because missionaries are willing to take in abandoned children, the infants are left at the missions.

THE YORUBA

The Yoruba are one of the major ethnic groups of Nigeria, Benin, and Togo. In Benin they make up about 12 percent of the population. Most of them live in the southeast of the country. In Benin the Yoruba are sometimes referred to as the Nago or Nagot people.

In Yoruba tradition, their kingdoms were begun by the sons of Oduduwa. These sons came down to earth from heaven and founded the Yoruba kingdom at Ife. Ife is in modern-day Nigeria and was a thriving city from the 12th to 15th centuries. Even after that, when its power declined, it remained a spiritual center for the Yoruba.

Yoruba families are very close, and children know their extended families on both sides very well. People often feel as though they were raised by the whole family, not just their parents. Neighbors also help each other in caring for one another's children.

Women in Yoruba culture customarily lose their own names upon the birth of their first child. If the first child was named John, the woman would thereafter be known as Mama-John. Children are given an official naming ceremony when they are 8 days old. Superstition says that if a child is not named at this time, he or she will die before his or her parent of the same sex. For the naming ceremony, guests bring gifts for the child. Ritual foods are offered to the baby, and he or she is given a bit of everything to taste. Members of the gathering offer prayers on the baby's behalf and may sing hymns. Then the baby's name is announced. Afterward everyone enjoys an evening of music and dancing to celebrate.

Names are very important to the Yoruba. A person's name is believed to have the power to influence his or her behavior and destiny. So a family will choose a name carefully, considering its meaning and their own family traditions. Some families believe the child comes with his or her name and it is their job to divine what that name is.

The Yoruba of Ife left behind such wonderful art that some 20th century explorers wondered if Ife was the lost city of Atlantis!

NAMING A YORUBA CHILD

Parents may name their child after his or her father's occupation or the circumstances of the birth. A hunter, who uses equipment like a gun or spear made of iron, may name a child Ogunbunmi, which means "Ogun (the god of iron) gave me this." The firstborn of twins may be named Taiwo ("taster of the world"), while the secondborn may be named Kehinde ("late arrival"). The traditional name for a child born to a mother who has had a pair of twins is Idowu, and the child born after that may be named Alaba if it is a girl or Idogbe if it is a boy. A baby born in the breech position may be named Ige, while the names Ojo (for a boy) and Aina (for a girl) are traditional for babies born with the umbilical cord wrapped around the neck. A child born with curly hair might be named Dada.

Children may be named after the day of the week on which they were born, or they may be named Abiodun (if born on a festival day) or Bosede (if born on a holy day). If a female family member died shortly before the birth of a girl, the child may be named Yetunde ("she has come back"). If a male family member had died shortly before the birth of a

Children have a special place in Beninois culture and choosing the correct name for one's child is a serious matter.

boy, the baby may be named Babatunde ("he has come back"). Another traditional name is Tokunbo, which signifies that the parents were out of the country when the child was born.

THE FON

The Fon make up almost 40 percent of Benin's population. They mostly live in the southern and central areas of the country. During the French occupation many Fon found work in the civil service. Since then, many have emigrated to other French-speaking areas of Africa.

THE FON AND TWINS

Among the Fon, the birth of twins is considered very special and is a welcome event. Children who are twins are treated more carefully than other children. They are always dressed alike, and gifts to one child must

Twins are regarded as two parts of a single being and are referred to by the phrase "he who comes divided."

Benin is a land where people of many ethnic groups coexist. These groups speak different languages and have different customs, yet things such as marriage and the naming of children hold a special place for all of them.

also be given to the other. If one twin dies, the mother must carry a wooden image of the dead twin with her at all times and care for it. Gifts to the surviving twin must be duplicated so that the dead twin receives every gift the live twin receives. Once both twins have died, *hovi* (statues that represent the twins) are carved for them.

NAMING A FON CHILD

Names are also very important in Fon culture. As soon as a woman knows she is pregnant, she will take note of significant events in her life and weigh what they might mean in relation to the baby and the name he or she should have. Even small events such as whom she meets in the market or whom she speaks with when she fetches water could be important.

Newborns are examined for things like birthmarks or deformities, the position in which they exited the womb is noted, and even whether they cry is important enough to take note of. Children may be named after the day of the week on which they were born, or by some attribute they were born with, or by birth order.

Sometimes the circumstances of labor and delivery are important. If a woman goes into labor on her way to the market, she might name her child Alifoe ("man of the road") or Alipossi ("girl of the road").

OTHER ETHNIC GROUPS

Many ethnic groups exist in Benin, but their members are not as numerous as the Fon, the Yoruba, or the Bariba. Two of these groups are the Somba and the Fulani.

The Somba primarily live in the northwestern part of the country in the Atakora Mountains and build two-storied windowless houses. The lack of windows is designed to keep intruders out. Because of their elaborate houses, the Somba are sometimes called "castle peasants." The lower floor of the house is used to stable animals and for storage, while the family lives on the second floor. A shrine near the entrance of the house honors the ancestors of that family's lineage.

The soil in the area in which they live is very poor and the Somba themselves tend to stay isolated from others. However, to bring more income to their villages, they have begun to entice tourists to their villages during times of celebrations and dances. Approximately 72,000 Somba live in Benin. Mattieu Kerekou, the former president, is one of the most well-known of the Somba.

A rural Somba village.

The Fulani are found throughout West Africa. All told, there are approximately 12 million of them, though only about 100,000 live in Benin. Most Fulani are nomadic cattleherders who are Muslim. The Islam practiced by the Fulani is a non-puritanical variety which has been influenced by the animist religions of their neighbors. The Fulani are also called the Peul or the Fulbé.

During the 19th century, the Fulani were engaged in a series of holy wars, which resulted in a far-flung but short-lived Fulani empire. Fulani legends claim they originated in Arabia and spread westward from there. The Fulani are lighter-skinned than their neighbors and have thin noses, lips, and slender builds.

LIFESTYLE

MOST PEOPLE in Benin live their lives bound by the traditions of their ancestors. Indeed, since their ancestors are still considered part of their lives, continuing their traditions is a way of respecting those who have died. People honor their ancestors and their traditions, though they may adopt some Western customs, such as white wedding dresses, if they wish to and feel that these customs add to their lives in some way. Benin is becoming a mixture of native and Western customs, a mixture that gives the country a complex and vibrant culture.

RURAL AND CITY LIFE

Most people in Benin live in small villages where they know everyone and follow the same traditions they have for centuries. Meals are taken on the floor, with the men separate from the women and children. A few people may have radios, but most do not have electricity, running water, or indoor plumbing. Showers and toilets are located outside the house. Streets are merely mud tracks through the forest or savanna and are often impassable when it rains. People do not own cars, but a few will operate taxis or scooters and take paying passengers along with them. Bus and postal service are somewhat regular but not always dependable.

Those who live in cities have better access to things such as electricity and indoor plumbing. They also have better access to medical care in hospitals and are more likely to be able to take a regular bus to work or the market. A higher percentage of their children will go to school and learn to read and write. Stores, gas stations, and hotels are located in the cities. Outside of the cities, people must bring their own gas from the cities or shop at the local markets for whatever they need. Lodging is hard to come by.

Above: **A look at Porto Novo, the official capital of Benin.**

Opposite: **The majority of Beninois live in small villages but an urban lifestyle with modern conveniences and Western influences is accessible to those living in cities.**

Life in Benin's small villages is starkly different from life in the cities.

People in the cities have often adopted a more Western style of dress and may eat as a family instead of eating with the men separate from the women and the children, as many do in the villages. And instead of using their hands as they eat on mats on the floor, people in the cities may use Western-style dining room furniture and utensils.

MARRIAGE

One of the main reasons for social gatherings is the celebration of a new marriage. Although people in Benin have adopted some Western customs such as white wedding dresses, most weddings in Benin still contain some aspect of long-respected traditions.

Among the Yoruba, the wedding ceremony itself is often largely Western in style. The bride wears a Western-style white dress, and the groom wears a suit. The ceremony takes place in a church with a reception following. For the reception, however, the couple will most likely have changed to traditional attire. Some Western music may be played at the reception, but traditional music is sure to be played as well.

FINDING A MATCH

Arranged marriages were common in the past but are less so now. But even if a couple is more modern in the sense that they chose each other rather than allow their families to hire a marriage broker for them, Yoruba marriages tend to be very traditional. The groom will be financially responsible for the family, while the bride will be the one who takes care of the house, the children, and her husband. In the past it was common for Yoruba men to have more than one wife, but due to economic circumstances that practice is less common today. Having large families with children very close in age has traditionally been very important to Yoruba men and women. But supporting more than one household, each with its own complement of children, can be very expensive! Today men who are having fewer wives and fewer children by choice are becoming more common.

Before the wedding, there are many traditional elements to a Yoruba wedding. For instance, before an official engagement, the groom's family will meet with the bride's family to officially ask permission for the daughter to marry their son. Several family members are traditionally part of this ceremony, including the groom and his immediate family; the bride and her immediate family; an *olopa iduro* (literally, "standing policeman"), who is a speaker appointed by the groom's family to present their request and who may be a family member or someone hired for the occasion; and an *olopa ijoko* (literally, "sitting policeman"), who represents the bride's family and who may be a family member or someone they have hired for the ceremony.

This ceremony takes place at the bride's house, and her family is traditionally responsible for the cost and for all preparations. If the groom's family is financially able, they may volunteer to help defray the costs associated with the ceremony. Although the Yoruba do not normally make much of punctuality, in the case of this introduction ceremony, the bride's family may cancel the event if the groom and his family are late.

Upon entering the bride's parents' home, the groom's female relatives kneel, and his male relatives prostrate themselves on the floor. Then the two families sit on opposite sides of the room while the *olopa iduro* and *olopa ijoko* sit in the center. The *olopa iduro* introduces everyone in the groom's family to the bride's family. He presents a letter from the family to the bride's family that formally requests the woman's hand in marriage. The

Marriage is an important aspect of adult life for Beninois, especially for the women, who will move to live with their husbands after the ceremony.

olopa iduro then hands the letter to the *olopa ijoko*, who reads it out loud, and the family responds immediately. Because the families have known for some time about the young couple's wish to marry, and the bride's family have made extensive preparations for this event, there is little risk of a negative answer at this stage. This is simply the time when the bride's family traditionally gives their blessing for the marriage to proceed.

At this time, it is traditional for the groom's family to present the bride's family with a gift (*owo-ori-iyawo*), and a prayer is offered. The *olopa iduro* and *olopa ijoko* then taste several traditional foods before offering them to everyone present. When kola nuts are shared, the families repeat the words, "*Won ma gbo. Won ma to. Won ma d'agba,*" which means, "They will ripen, they will eat and not go hungry, they will grow old."

Also eaten are fruits called *ata ire*. These contain many seeds. According to Yoruba tradition, the number of seeds that fall from the fruit will equal the number of children the couple will have. Honey (*oyin*), sugar, and sugarcane (*ireke*) are also eaten to symbolize that the marriage will be a sweet one.

To complete the ceremony, family members may make additional speeches, and the families may exchange additional gifts. Then it is time to eat the great banquet the bride's family prepared and listen to the singers and drummers who have been hired for the happy occasion.

Some time after the introduction ceremony, the couple will officially be engaged at a second ceremony. Everyone dresses in clothes made from traditional cloths called *aso oke*. Once again, the families meet at the bride's family's house, and her family purchases and prepares everything. Symbolic foods are presented to everyone, and gifts like a Bible or rings will be exchanged. During this ceremony the bride traditionally has her face covered.

Afterward everyone except the bride goes outside. She waits inside until she is called out. She will emerge from the house with her face still covered and kneel in front of her parents, who then offer a prayer on her behalf. After that, she will kneel before the groom's parents, who also pray for her. The bride then sits beside the groom and removes her veil.

The engagement ceremony is traditionally followed almost immediately by the wedding. After the wedding ceremony is over, and the reception has been held, the bride goes to the groom's house. She is supposed to arrive first so that she can receive her husband when he arrives home.

Some believe that the celebratory aspect of funeral rituals in many Beninois cultures can still be seen today, although in a changed form, in the upbeat jazz funerals of New Orleans.

DEATH

Because death marks the transition of the soul from one plane of existence to another, it is greeted with rejoicing by the family, especially if the person who died was very old. In the case of a death, although the family is grieving, they still want to express their joy that their relative has gone on to join the rest of the ancestors. The greater the age attained before death, the greater the celebration.

If a young person dies, however, especially if he or she was too young to have children, the funeral will be much less about celebrating the end of a long life and more about the loss to the family. Sometimes parents do not even attend the funeral of a child who died young. People often wish each other good fortune by saying, "May you never bury a child in your lifetime." While brighter colors may be worn at the funeral of an

Two women pray at a Christian cemetery.

old person, much darker and duller colors are chosen for the burial of a young person. To show unity, the entire family may dress in clothes made from the same cloth.

Because there are no funeral homes as there are in the United States, it is the responsibility of the family to prepare the body for burial. In rural areas the burial is usually performed quickly after death, since there is no way to preserve a body. A man or woman whose spouse has died will cut his or her hair and will usually stay at home for a 40-day period of mourning. Sometimes men will have a shorter period of mourning than women, depending on ethnicity, traditional family practice, and personal preference.

In some traditions, hair and fingernail clippings are taken from the deceased person to be used in a "second burial." The second burial is performed when everyone in the family has had time to get together and prepare elaborate rituals. Because the body had to be buried quickly, there may not have been time for everyone to gather or for preparations to have been made at the primary funeral. If a family anticipated a death for some time, or if they are wealthy, they may have the resources to perform both burials at once. But most people must take months, or even years, to prepare the second burial properly.

At the second funeral, the family wears clothing made from the same fabric. Everyone is fed and given *sodabi* (a kind of palm wine) and other beverages to drink, and musicians play all night long. People dance until the early hours of the morning.

In some traditions, it is believed the spirit of the dead person cannot move on to the land of the ancestors until the second burial is performed. The longer the family waits, the more time the unhappy spirit lingers. It may even eventually try to maim or kill its family members if it has not been properly sent on its way. For this reason, between the first and second burials, some people wear palm fronds or place fronds over the doorways of their homes to protect them from a vengeful spirit.

EDUCATION

Before 1960, when Benin was under the colonial rule of France, the educational system in the country was quite advanced. The large numbers of intellectuals, educated elite, and professionals who had been educated within the country gave it a reputation as being Africa's "Latin Quarter." The situation changed once independence was achieved, however.

Benin has seen its education system paralyzed by many student strikes; the strikes often occurred over issues such as stipends and living conditions as they did over political issues. The worst strikes took place in 1985 after the government repealed an agreement to guarantee state employment to all graduates.

Despite the student strikes that affected the education system in the past, many Beninois value education.

THE SCHOOL SYSTEM

School attendance has traditionally been very uneven, with most school attendees living in the south. In Cotonou more than 90 percent of children are in school, while the percentage is only 17 percent in the northwest. Many Beninois understand the importance of education and have worked hard to get as much as they can given where they live in the country.

The school year stretches from September or October to June or July. Within the school system, classes are taught in French, although English is introduced to many students early in their studies. This is important because while many of Benin's neighbors have French as their official language, the national language of its eastern neighbor, Nigeria, is English. Thus a knowledge of English is important for communication with one of Benin's closest trading partners and neighboring countries.

NURSERY AND PRIMARY SCHOOLS

Approximately 66 percent of the nursery schools in Benin are public, and the rest are private. Children are generally sent to nursery school at the age of 3 or 4 and spend two years there. Most nursery schools focus on activities that stimulate learning, creativity, and social development.

After two years in nursery school, a student will be enrolled in primary school. Primary education begins at the age of 5 or 6 and is compulsory. Primary school is divided into three levels, and the students spend two years at each level: preparatory, elementary, and middle classes. Roughly 92 percent of the primary schools in the country are public, and the rest are private.

A teacher goes through the schoolwork of some students at a private elementary school.

Education for these young children will pave the way for a brighter future for all Beninois.

During primary school, students learn a variety of subjects: mathematics, writing (in French), reading comprehension, science, history and geography, art (singing, drawing, gardening), sports, and civic education. The curriculum is the same for every school across the country, and all students must pass the National Examination to graduate. If students pass this exam, they receive a certificate called the Certificat d'Étude Primaire (CEP). The exam is difficult, and students compete for the best grades, because the grades determine their place on a list for admission to secondary school.

SECONDARY SCHOOL

Secondary school in Benin covers seven years. These seven years are divided into two periods called cycles. The division between the first and the second cycle occurs after the fourth year of instruction.

The first two years of secondary school are largely the same for all students. They are taught French, mathematics, physics, chemistry, natural science, history, geography, English, home economics, computers, sports, and either German or Spanish. In the third year, however, students begin to take different coursework to emphasize one of three directions their education may go: literature, science, or a classical curriculum where the student studies Greek and Latin. At the end of the first cycle, the student takes a national exam called the Brevet d'Études du Premier Cycle (BEPC).

The curriculum of the second cycle is largely the same as the first, with the addition of philosophy. The student has four options to choose from during this cycle: literature, economics, mathematics, and biology. At the end of the second cycle the student takes a test called the Baccalaureat Exam (BAC). In 2000, 29 percent of students passed the BAC.

In 1998 more than 68 percent of students passed their National Examination.

UNIVERSITY

The main university in Benin is the National University of Benin (UNB), which encompasses 19 institutions on six campuses. It was founded in 1970. Prior to 1970, Beninois went to college in France or attended Senegal's Dakar University. Other universities in Benin are the University of Parakou and the University of Abomey-Calavi.

Enrollment in university-level education is growing quickly. In 1970 the enrollment at the university was 350. By 1995 that number had increased to 11,007. For the 1998–99 school year enrollment was 16,284.

A secondary-school degree is required before a student can get into the university. Those who wish to apply for scholarships or other financial support must take a special entrance examination.

RELIGION

THE BENINOIS are very spiritual people who display deep faith in their traditional religion, which is vodun. Vodun is an animistic religion, which means that its followers believe that every animal, plant, and thing (such as mountains, rocks, and streams) has a spirit, created by a remote all-powerful god. Very powerful spirits can bring good or bad luck and can be influenced by prayers and sacrifices in their honor. People worship these spirits at shrines as the protectors of the natural world in which they live.

FREEDOM OF RELIGION

The constitution of Benin guarantees religious freedom for its citizens. Government officials show their respect to prominent members of all religions by attending religious celebrations to which they are invited. The president of the country is expected to meet with religious leaders of all faiths, and police forces are expected to provide security to any religious group which requests it. Benin's Constitutional Court has ruled that it is unconstitutional for people to block access to others' religious services and that religious groups could not deny others access to public facilities. This was determined after a vodun priest attempted to deny Christians access to a public lake on the grounds that the lake was religious property.

Anyone wishing to form a religious group must register their group with the Ministry of the Interior. All groups must meet the same registration requirements. According to the International Religious Freedom Report 2005, there is no evidence that any religious groups in Benin have been refused permission to register or have been subject to unusual delays or harassments during registration. No reports have been made of forced conversions from one religion to another, or of terrorist attacks on religious organizations, or of people being detained or imprisoned due to their religion.

Because the state does not promote one religion over another, religion is not taught to children in the public schools. However, religious groups may establish their own schools.

Opposite: **In Benin, the everyday lives of the people are greatly influenced by religion. Here, a man on motorcycle guides a Zangbeto masked dancer through the village. The Zangbeto masquerade is an important event held during the dry season to appease ancestral spirits.**

73

Religious tolerance is widely practiced in Benin, possibly because of the diversity of religions which may be found not only within communities but also within families. It would not be unusual for one family to consist of Christians, Muslims, and followers of vodun. In fact, Christians and Muslims frequently practice those religions in addition to practicing vodun.

Interfaith dialogue is common. The first Wednesday in May is celebrated as Ecumenical Day, in which religious leaders travel to Ouidah to speak about interfaith tolerance and attempt to bridge the divide between followers of different religions.

National holidays include Christian holidays such as Christmas, Muslim holidays such as the Prophet Mohammad's birthday, and Vodun Day.

Ritual objects are often used during vodun ceremonies, for example the doll and shells used by this woman at a religious ceremony.

VODUN

Every January 10 since 1992, the people of Benin celebrate their national religion on Vodun Day. Vodun can also be spelled "vodoun," but it is more commonly known in the West as voodoo. This religion came to the New World on slave ships, but it originated in the area that is now Benin and Nigeria.

People who follow vodun may also consider themselves Catholics or Muslims, as all these religions believe in a god who created the world, as well as in lesser spirits, both good and evil, who can influence the lives of the people. All three religions profess belief in an afterlife. Therefore, it is common for people to practice two religions without viewing them to be in conflict.

There are many versions of vodun in Benin, but the two main ones are vodun, practiced by the Fon people, and orisha, practiced by the Yoruba. For the Yoruba the main god is Olorun, while for the Fon the creator god is Mawu. Mawu may also be known as Dada-Segbo, Semedo, or Gbedoto, depending on the aspect of his being the person wishes to emphasize. For instance, if one is interested in emphasizing Mawu's creation of life, he would be referred to as Gbedoto.

Priests of vodun can be male (*houngan*) or female (*manbo*). The initiates they train to become priests are called *vodunsi*. The priest serves a particular spirit in a temple with an altar in the center. The altar can be decorated with many items, including candles, and items that represent

Priestesses dancing at a vodun ceremony, dressed in elaborate costumes.

THE VODUN AND ORISHA

The supreme god of vodun and orisha is considered to be too infinite and remote for ordinary human beings to deal with, and he is not actually worshiped. For their needs, humans must appeal to and appease spirits closer to hand. These spirits were created by the supreme being and are above all natural laws; their reponsibilities include interacting with humans. They are the ones to receive worship from living people. They have nothing to do with the dead, except to deliver their souls to the creator god.

People worship thousands of spirits, but the seven most important in vodun, all considered sons of Mawu, are the following:

Sakpata, the eldest son, who has been given lordship over the earth. People are afraid of him because of his terrible power. Symbols of his power include scissors, chains, and smallpox. He has many sons, including Ada Tangni, the spirit of leprosy, and Sinji Aglosumato, the spirit of incurable sores.

Xevioso is the lord of the sky and of thunder. He is responsible for punishing liars and criminals. His symbols include a double-headed axe, lightning, fire, and the color red.

Agbe is lord of the sea. His symbol is a serpent.

Gu is lord of war and iron. He is responsible for giving technology to people, as well as for punishing accomplices to doers of evil deeds.

Age is lord of agriculture, animals, and forests.

Jo is invisible and is lord of the air.

Legba is the youngest son. After his other brothers were given lordship over various things, nothing was left over for him. Legba was jealous of his brothers and became the spirit of unpredictability.

In orisha, some of the main spirits worshiped are Shango, a sky spirit who rules storms and lightning; Erinle, the spirit of the forest; Agwe, the spirit of the ocean; Oko, the spirit governing agriculture; and Ezili, the spirit of love. The most popularly worshiped of these is Shango because he is believed to be the father of the Yoruba themselves. Shango's symbols are a double-headed axe and the color red, so he is very similar in that respect to the Fon god Xevioso.

the spirit. Several times a year, the *vodunsi* may go into the streets of a village, dancing to drums and wearing elaborate costumes. These ceremonies are held whenever required or wanted and do not conform to a set schedule.

Training to become a vodun priest takes place at a special school. The students live a life of simplicity and must endure trials that test their strength and their resolve. They must memorize their lessons and repeat them back to the teachers exactly. The students must learn chants, dances, and secrets of their religion, which may not be revealed to outsiders. Other tasks for the students include making masks, baskets, and cloth, which are sold at the market. Students are not allowed to be idle; their hours are filled with work or study.

Upon graduation, the young priests are urged to be responsible to the land, the spirits, their ancestors, and their fellow priests. Each is given a handful of sand from his or her native land to emphasize where his or her responsibilities lie.

Vodun encompasses magic, both good and bad. Good magic (*bo*) exists in the form of spells or charms that turn away evil. Evil magic (*aze*) harms people. Sorcerers who practice evil sorcery are despised.

A vodun follower dressed in an elaborate costume on Vodun Day.

DIVINATION AND INITIATION

Each person has a destiny attached to him or her before birth. The Fon call this *fa*, and the Yoruba call it *ori*. People must go to a diviner to discover this destiny. The diviner is called *bokono* by the Fon and *babalao* by the Yoruba. A person who has a question about his or her life, past, present, or future, can go to a diviner, who will throw seed pods or cowrie shells to find the answers. Spirits who look after the person will control the pattern into which the pods or shells fall so that the diviner can read the message that the spirits want conveyed.

Initiation into the religion is gradual and takes place at various times during a person's life. Shortly after birth, a child will be presented to the family and community (this includes the deceased ancestors) in a ceremony called *agabasa-yiyi*. The name of this ritual consists of the words

A shrine to Olokun at a Fon village.

for the front room of the house, *agbasa*, and the word for receiving or reception, *yiyi*. At this ceremony the diviner will reveal the destiny of the child, as well as the *joto* (deceased ancestor) whose personality animates the child. This *joto* is not a spirit, because the dead ancestors have gone on to another realm, called Yesunyime. But an aspect of the personality of the dead is left behind, to continue to live from family member to family member in the form of their *joto*. This *joto* will be the protector (*se*) of the child. Once the *joto* is recognized, it is welcomed back to the family with the phrase, *"Se doo nu we"* (*"Se, we welcome you"*).

The signs that reveal the *joto* are called the *du*. This is referred to as "the word of the oracle." The *du* is entrusted to the parents, especially the mother, to keep for the child until he or she is older. Each *du* has its own particular rules that must be followed. For instance, a *du* may forbid certain foods to be eaten by those whom it protects. So the mother would not fix those foods for the children with that *du*, but when they are older, around 12 or 13, the children would be informed of *du* and held responsible for avoiding these foods themselves. At that age, children are considered *do so kan nu*, or mature enough to take on the responsibility for their own destiny.

The *agabasa-yiyi* ritual is extremely important. It ties the baby not only to his living family but also to the ancestors who have gone before and to the *du* that will govern and direct his or her life. Those who have never had this ritual performed for them do not have status in the community. Without *du* and *joto* to tie them to the living, the dead, destiny, and the community at large, they are people without roots. If people suspect that someone has not gone through this ritual, they will feel compelled to inquire whether or not it has been performed.

At around the age of 20, men and women are initiated into another stage of vodun through a ritual called *fa-sinsen* or *fa-yiyi*, the Receiving of the *fa*. Young people are presumed to be troubled by their *fa* and must make a public declaration of their reception and devotion to it in order to find personal harmony; youthful rebelliousness and freedom come under adult self-control. Once again, a diviner is consulted, and this time an animal is sacrificed in order to clear the young person's path of obstacles and misfortunes.

OLOKUN

Olokun is a spirit widely worshiped in West Africa who may be male or female, depending on the culture. Among the Yoruba, Olokun is female and is the wife of Olorun, the creator god. She is the mother of all bodies of water.

Olokun rules over history, the future, visions, patience, and endurance. She is also responsible for material wealth and mental health and is especially concerned with women who desire children. Because Olokun has governance over the ocean, those who were taken away during the slave trade are thought to be under her patronage. Olokun works closely with Oya, the spirit of sudden changes, and people's ancestors to help people negotiate the transition between life and death. Politicians often gravitate to Olokun, as she is responsible for helping people rise in the political and social spheres.

Here's a prayer to Olokun:

"I praise the spirit of the vast ocean;

I praise the spirit of the ocean who is beyond understanding;

Spirit of the ocean, I will worship you as long as there is water in the sea;

Let there be peace in the ocean, let there be peace in my soul.

Spirit of the ocean, ageless one, I give respect. May it be so."

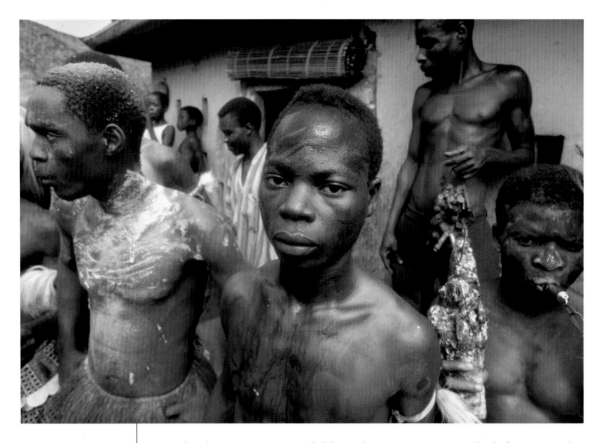

Young men at a vodun ceremony. Their faces and bodies are painted as part of the rites.

A third initiation is available only to men. It is called *fa-tite*, or the Consultation of the *fa*. A candidate applies for a consultation in order to receive the entire revelation of his destiny. This initiation ceremony takes place in the forest and cannot be observed by women or non-initiated men. The diviner once again throws nuts or shells in order to discover what knowledge the spirits have to pass on concerning the initiate. If the signs are positive, everyone present rejoices. If the signs are negative, animals are sacrificed in order to ward off the death, illness, poverty, and despair that may be coming to the individual as part of his destiny. The initiate takes a bath in flowing water to cleanse himself after the ceremony, and parts of his body, such as bits of hair and fingernails, are buried in the forest to symbolize the initiate's desire to cast away impurity. After this, the initiate goes home confident he knows the meaning of his own life, his own personal destiny completely revealed.

SHRINES

Humans communicate with the divine in vodun or orisha through shrines. Shrines come in many forms. They may be something natural, such as a clearing in a forest or a tree, or they can be something man-made, such as a building or a stick poked into the ground. The landscape of the entire country is filled with such shrines, which people have set aside and erected to ensure that they have the ability to reach the spirits.

The shrine is the point where two worlds—the world of spirits and the world of people—meet. At its spiritual center is an altar where people will place sacrifices, such as alcohol, money, or food. People may do this for their personal benefit or may gather as families or communities in order to worship and petition for the things they desire.

One ritual that often takes place at shrines is spiritual possession. Worshipers believe they are possessed by spirits. Others may then have the opportunity to talk to the spirit directly through the medium of the possessed person.

Sometimes particular vodun or orisha prefer certain kinds of shrines over others. Among the Yoruba, the shrines of the god Ogun, who is lord of war, iron, and hunting, are often based around living trees that have the lower branches trimmed away. A woven garment like a skirt is placed onto the tree; it is called "the dress of Ogun." At the base of the tree, iron staffs are driven into the ground, since this is the metal sacred to the god. Smaller shrines not placed around trees may simply be two pieces of iron driven into the ground. The shrine becomes sacred when palm oil is poured onto it.

Several fetish items protect a house in Koussou Kouangou.

Rituals to Ogun often involve iron bells and machetes, which are used during his ceremonies and, when not in use, can be seen near the shrine. Ogun represents both destructive and creative forces. To appease his destructive nature, which is symbolized by the color red, people offer Ogun sacrificial blood, usually from the animals sacred to Ogun: the tortoise, the snail, and the dog. To appeal to Ogun's creative side, worshipers offer palm wine. By doing these things, people hope to keep destructive forces from entering their own lives, especially through any sort of industry or accident involving cars, guns, knives, mechanical equipment, or anything else made of metal.

Though many Beninois have converted to Islam or Christianity, they also practice some form of native religion such as vodun or orisha. These religions are central to people's lives. By worshiping and offering sacrifices to the spirits, these people express a spirituality and depth of faith that helps them cope with a complicated and rapidly changing world.

CATHOLIC MISSIONS

The first Catholic missionaries to reach Benin arrived in 1634. The missionaries set up operations in Ouidah. However, deaths from disease and the resistance of the locals to the missionaries' message doomed the original effort. Only sporadic efforts—all failures—occurred over the next two centuries.

The first successful Catholic mission was established in 1860 and was headed by Father Francois Borghero. Catholic schools were opened at the same time. Catholicism did not reach the north of the country unil 1937.

In 1965 an estimated 45 percent of all Beninois children who were attending school attended Catholic institutions. Later, most of these schools were absorbed into the state school system.

CHRISTIANITY

Christianity was originally brought to Benin by missionaries. Since these missionaries arrived by sea, it is no surprise that most of Benin's Christians live in the south of the country. Many of them live in Cotonou. Nearly half of all Beninois Christians belong to the Roman Catholic faith. The others belong to a wide variety of Christian groups such as Baptists, Jehovah's Witnesses, Assemblies of God, Seventh-day Adventists, and Mormons.

Missionaries continue to operate through the country. Christian denominations which are known to have missionaries in Benin include the Baptists, Church of the Nazarene, Assemblies of God, Mennonites, and Mormons, among others.

ISLAM

Islam arrived in Benin with Arab merchants who came across the Sahara with their goods. Thus, most of the Muslims in the country live in the north. Beninois Muslims are Sunnis. The few Shi'a who live in Benin are generally expatriates from abroad.

The Eglise Celeste is one of Benin's indigenous Christian sects.

LANGUAGE

MANY LANGUAGES are spoken in Benin. The one language people have in common is the national language, French, which is taught at home and in the schools. But around their own villages, people speak their native languages. The native languages of Benin are not written languages, so any time one wishes to write something down, it must be in French. The languages native of Benin are tonal, which means that the tone with which words are spoken influences the meaning. This is very difficult for speakers of English to learn. It is often easier for visitors to try to communicate in French rather than to try a native language, but most people are eager to teach you their own language if you are interested.

Above: **A small billboard in French advertises the services of a hairdressing salon.**

Opposite: **A signboard in French reflects the emphasis of Beninois on self-reliance and diligence. French is the only written language in Benin.**

GBE

One of the main language families in Benin is Gbe. This family includes the languages of the Ewe, the Adja, and the Fon. It is a small part of the Niger-Congo family of languages, which are spoken all across West Africa. Tradition claims that Gbe speakers originated much farther east than their present-day locations in Benin and Togo, but that Yoruba attacks between the 10th and 13th centuries sent them fleeing westward. Gbe speakers then founded the kingdom of Tado, which today would be located in the country of Togo. Other Gbe speakers left Tado to form other kingdoms in later centuries, including the kingdom of Allada, which for a time was the capital of the Fon people.

By 1850 the slave trade with Europe had nearly disappeared. Missionaries brought Christianity to the area. These missionaries began to produce dictionaries and grammar books that recorded many local dialects of the

Gbe languages. Though they were not without mistakes, these efforts began to display the wealth of languages and dialects the area nurtured. Since then, many scholars have advanced the West's knowledge of the Gbe languages.

Gbe languages have several things in common. Perhaps the strangest thing for speakers of English or other European languages is that Gbe languages, like all other native Benin languages, are tonal. Most of them display three tones: high, mid, and low, although in many dialects the lower two are not differentiated by native speakers. Tonal languages use

French is the language of instruction in all schools.

the pitch of the word to convey its meaning. Thus two words may be spelled the same and pronounced the same but have different pitches, and so are different words with different meanings.

Children learn the tones of their native language by copying the adults around them. Interestingly, children often learn the tones of their language before anything else. But speakers of non-tonal languages who attempt to learn a tonal language as adults may have a great deal of trouble in hearing and interpreting the different tones.

In tonal languages, the pitch rather than the stress on the word and its syllables may change or subtly shift its meaning. In Igala, a tonal language

FON WORDS AND PHRASES

A do gangi a?	Are you well?
Eeen, un do gangi.	Yes, I am well.
Kudo zan zan.	Good morning.
Kudo hweme.	Good afternoon.
Kudo gbada.	Good evening.
Bo yi bo wa.	Go and come back (good-bye).
Ma yi bo wa.	I will go and come back (the response to the previous phrase).
No	Mother
Novi	Brother or sister (another child of one's mother)
To	Father
Keke	Bicycle
Zungbo	The forest
Avokanfun	Cotton
Ajinaku	Elephant
Agonde	Pineapple
Nukplonmeto	Teacher
Blo dede.	Be careful.

of Nigeria, the word *awo* can mean "to slap," "guinea fowl," "hole in a tree," "comb," "star," or "increase," depending on tone.

Gbe languages generally have a sentence structure similar to that of English, with the basic sentence being subject-verb-object, as in, "the boy threw the ball." When it comes to verb tense, however, Gbe languages are different from English, distinguishing only between present and future. Past tense must be understood through context or by the placement of special adverbs that describe the definite end of an action.

Questions in Gbe languages often require what is called a question marker. This is a special word that changes the sentence from a statement to a question. In Fon this is a final *a* added to the end of the question. "*A se Fongbe a?*" means "Do you speak Fon?"

YORUBA

Yoruba is another language spoken in Benin. Most, though not all, of its 300 dialects are actually spoken in Nigeria. It is part of the Benue-Congo

branch of the Niger-Congo language family. Yoruba is tonal like the Gbe
languages. In Yoruba, the word *igba* might mean "half a calabash," "two
hundred," or "locust tree," depending on tone.

When you greet others in Yoruba, it is important to note the relative
age of the person to whom you are speaking. If you are speaking to
someone your age or younger, you will use one greeting. If you are
speaking to someone older, you will use a different form. When saying
"good morning" to someone your age or younger, you would say "*ku
aro*"; to someone older, "*e ku aro.*"

Not all phrases have two forms, however. Sometimes the same phrase
will be used no matter the age of the person to whom you are speaking.
For instance, "goodbye" is always *odabo*, "yes" is always *be ni*, "no" is
always *oti*, and "good night" is always *o di aro.*

THE PRESS

For many years after the 1972 coup, Benin had only one newspaper,
Ehuzu, which was styled as a voice for the socialist revolution. The regime
found itself embarrassed, however, during a newspaper exposition in
Europe attended by Kerekou. His country's submission of *Ehuzu* made
it obvious that Benin lacked the kind of newspaper other countries had.

A small printing press in Benin. The printing equipment in these companies are usually old and basic.

Most of *Ehuzu* was taken up with mentions of Kerekou's itinerary, and it reported very little actual news.

One of Kerekou's companions on the trip decided that Benin could do better. He applied for permission to print another daily paper, and after two years, he finally received approval. He went to Nigeria and Cameroon to study the independent newspapers that were thriving there at the time, then returned to Benin ready to begin publishing. His paper, *La Gazette*, was immensely popular, with its first issue selling out within seven hours. However, Kerekou's government was unhappy with the paper's ambitions of reporting news that was not flattering to the government, and government censors began to cut out articles. Issues of *La Gazette* ran with blank spaces where articles should have been.

After socialism was abandoned, many other newspapers started in Benin, but few thrived. Between 1988 and 1996, more than 170 newspapers had been registered at the office of the interior ministry. For a time, a paper called *La Recade* prided itself on being similar to the newspapers that had been published under colonial rule. The name *La Recade* referred to the baton carried by a messenger of the king that established the authority of the messenger and his message. In the end, however, even *La Recade* ceased publication.

The perils of trying to publish a newspaper in a country where the literacy rate is low are many. It is difficult for newspapers to sell enough advertising to support themselves, and the equipment they have to work with is old and often broken. Print runs are small, at about 3,000 to 3,500 copies, and the paper is poor in quality. Photos cannot be reproduced well with the equipment available and are usually blurry. Journalists are often college graduates who were unable to find a job in law or economics right after graduation and who see journalism as a temporary job. Despite these difficulties, some journalists in Benin are staying with the profession and writing news stories that matter. Their efforts are paying off: In the late 1990s, New York-based Freedom House rated only two countries in Africa as having a free press. Benin was one of them.

ARTS

THE PEOPLE of Benin have a wide variety of traditions involving the arts, such as music and storytelling and weaving, which are important parts of their daily lives. Some traditions, like that of the storytellers called *griots*, were once the reserve of royalty, but now *griots* wander the countryside, bringing their tales to anyone who wishes to listen. Some traditions, such as the weaving of *kijipa* cloth by the Yoruba, are fading from fashion, but new traditions, such as acting or writing, are taking hold. Today Benin is becoming part of the worldwide academic and entertainment arena, to everyone's benefit.

MUSIC

Among the Yoruba, the most important musical instruments are the drums. An iron bell may be used in music dedicated to Ogun, the spirit of iron, and a gourd rattle is often added to music dedicated to Shango, spirit of thunder. But for the most part, drums make up the music of the Yoruba.

One form of music is the *bata* ensemble. Several kinds of drums make up the ensemble. They are the *omele ako* ("male small drum"), the *omele abo* ("female small drum"), the *eki*, and the *iya ilu* ("mother drum"). The first three perform most of the structure of each piece, while the mother drum plays a different but supporting rhythm. The *omele ako* may interact with the rest of its section or change to match the mother drum at times.

Yoruba in other countries and their descendants in the New World have similar ensembles, but the Benin *bata* groups are unique. Their

Above: **Drums are prevalent in the music of Benin, and *bata* drum players create a very distinctive sound.**

Opposite: **The music and dances of Benin are unique art forms.**

iya ilu and *omele ako* have much lower pitches than those of drums in Nigeria or Brazil. Also, the *eki* is not used elsewhere.

Bata ensembles are used during *egungun* rituals. During a Shango ceremony, the *elegun* (initiates) begin dancing in the afternoon around a tree where three *bata* players are located. Male dancers form an outer circle, and female dancers form an inner circle. Women dance with bodies leaning forward and arms down, taking small steps to the rhythm of the drums. Men dance with longer strides and lift their arms to touch their hands over their heads, then let their arms fall down to their sides with a loud slap. Sometimes the men dance more acrobatically, guided by the drums. The rhythm of the drums is short, sharp, and strident in order to remind people of the nature of Shango.

In Benin, women performers are an integral part of music and dance ensembles.

Another sort of drumming group is the *dundun* ensemble, which in Benin is often referred to as *gangan*. This ensemble contains an *iya ilu* solo bass drum, which for this ensemble is called a *dundun* drum. It is an hourglass-shape instrument. The membranes of the drum are pierced by a leather string, which the musician can use to change the tension in the drum. In other ensembles, the *iya ilu* also has strings, but they are left free. Another drum in this ensemble is the *keri keri*, which has a higher pitch and is played by being struck with either a hand or a stick. The other drums in this ensemble are the *omele*, the *asasu*, and *gudugudu*. The *gudugudu* has only one membrane and is played with two small leather sticks.

Music is an integral part of daily life in Benin and is indispensable during rituals for vodun and orisha. The instruments have their own sounds, names, and parts to play in the various ensembles that make up Benin's musical tradition.

Music is an inseparable component of Beninois culture, accompanying festivals, rituals, and daily activities.

The best tobacc
money can buy

Rothmans

WEAVING

Textiles has always been central to much of Yoruba social and religious life. The Yoruba tell the story of how, in the beginning, people went about naked and were always arguing. The spirit Eshu decided to do something about that, so he taught men to harvest cotton, weave it into cloth, and wear it. When the other people saw the cloth, they responded with respect, and social harmony came to people for the first time.

Women use an upright loom to make a traditional indigo-and-white striped cloth called *kijipa*. A woman would recruit her sisters and daughters to help her spin the thread to be used in the loom. *Kijipa* cloth was widely traded to the north via overland routes and to Europeans on the coast who sold them in the Gold Coast (modern-day Ghana), the Congo, and Brazil.

Other ceremonial cloths were made in local patterns and styles using the upright loom. If the cloth was particularly important to certain rituals, a man might have woven it, though men did not generally use the upright loom. Today few weavers of either gender still use the upright loom.

Most of the cloth woven by men is produced on a narrow-strip loom that was originally imported into the Yoruba region from the north via the overland trade routes. Today the colors and styles of the Yoruba weavers reflect recent fashions, but three traditional cloths are still made. They are *etu*, *sanyan*, and *alaari*. Together these traditional cloths of the Yoruba are referred to as *aso oke*.

Etu cloth is of a blue that is so dark that the threads used to weave it had to be immersed many times in the indigo dye. The dark color is offset by lighter threads that make stripes sometimes only one thread in width. *Etu* means "guinea fowl," and the cloth is supposed to resemble the speckled feathers of the bird. A person who wears *etu* is one who is well respected, and there is a Yoruba proverb saying that a man who wears an *etu*-cloth cap on his head will never again have to carry anything for himself.

Sanyan cloth is beige and is made from the silk of the Anaphe moth. The silk is undyed, so the beige color can be uneven. The final cloth often has a white stripe in the center of each woven strip.

Ritual cloths like aso oke *are worn for weddings, birthdays, a baby's naming ceremony, engagements, funerals, and religious festivals.*

Left: **Weaving is an activity undertaken by men and women alike.**

Opposite: **This merchant is part of the revitalized textile industry in Benin.**

Alaari cloth is made using a magenta-dyed silk imported from across the Sahara. Because it had to be imported over a great distance, this cloth was always extremely rare, and entire outfits of it were rarer still. Usually small bits of *alaari* would be used as stripes in a cloth produced locally.

One shift that has occurred during the past century is that the consumers for *aso oke* are no longer the royal and other important families but rather the educated elite of the cities. They set a fashion still popular today, in which groups of people at celebratory events express their unity by wearing outfits in the same cloth. The demand for *aso oke* has meant a revitalization of the weaving industry and has required so many weavers that women have joined the men as producers of *aso oke*.

These boys operate a narrow-strip loom commonly found in the Yoruba region, producing traditional cloths as well as more modern designs.

FILM

In 1998 Belgian director Dominique Loreau released the film *Divine Carcasse*, which was set in Benin. The story revolves around the fact that for the French character in the film, the word "ancestor" is used for old, decrepit things such as his ancient car, but to the Africans around him, the word refers to the mysterious forces that are always present and that shape their lives.

The European character Simon imports his old car to the country, but it is not reliable, and he gets rid of it by giving it to Joseph, a Beninois man. Joseph feels that the old car will be key to starting a taxi business that will help him succeed. His fellow villagers are envious that Joseph has a car, especially when he tells them that it is referred to in French as an "ancestor." Joseph's wife is wary of her neighbors' envy and asks for the protection of her own ancestors. But during an *egungun* ritual, Joseph's ancestors tell him the car is cursed by a recently deceased uncle. He must get rid of it.

The last part of the film follows the car to another village, where there is a metalworker. In his shop the car is turned from a means of transportation into an object with magical powers: a fetish which is used to protect the village. After the villagers accept the fetish, they retreat to their homes, but the car remains with the village's other fetishes. As darkness falls, the car appears to have glowing eyes, as if it has been awakened and now sees in the dark its role as protector.

In this movie, the car can be seen as a symbol for one of the main ways in which Europe and Africa have interacted. Europe has brought its technology, often old and deteriorating, far behind what exists at home and Africans have incorporated it into their own beliefs and traditions.

The busy traffic and fast-developing cities are the result of the interaction between Benin and the Western world, a situation that has been depicted both positively and negatively in several films.

BENINOIS IN HOLLYWOOD

One actor from Benin who has achieved a measure of success in Hollywood is Djimon Hounsou (*below, right*). Hounsou emigrated to France in 1977 at age 13 and worked as a model for fashion designer Thierry Mugler. Eventually his modeling jobs opened up acting opportunities for him. His first major film role was in the movie *Stargate*. Since then he has had major roles in movies such as *Amistad*, *Gladiator*, *The Four Feathers*, *Beauty Shop*, and *The Island*. In 2003 he and Charlize Theron, who is from South Africa, were the first Africans to ever be nominated for an Academy Award. Hounsou was nominated for his work in the movie *In America*.

Beninois are becoming more well known in the international arts and entertainment industries. Angelique Kidjo, for example, has won numerous international awards for her music.

In the end, the car does no one any good as a car, but when the villagers, especially the metalworker, apply their resources and time and effort to it, it becomes something useful within the context of village life.

LITERATURE AND PHILOSOPHY

In 2005 female journalists from several west African countries were top winners in the Akintola Fatoyinbo Africa Education Journalism Awards, which were established in 2001. More than 700 articles were entered into the contest, and the quality was such that the coordinator of the African Association for the Development Education in Africa (ADEA), Professor Alfred Opubor, praised the entries.

An entry from Benin, "*La Fonction Enseignante la Vocation se Meurt*" ("*The Teaching Profession: The Call Is Dying*"), was written by Rose Akakpo and was originally published in *Le Point au Quotidien*. It won first prize over all other French-language entries. Akakpo had also won first prize in the French-language competition at the first awards ceremony in September 2002 for the article "*Revaloriser la Fonction Enseignante*" ("*Raising the Prestige of Teaching*"), which was also originally published in *Le Point au Quotidien*.

One Beninois who has had a varied career as an author, philosopher, and politician is Paulin J. Hountondji. He was born in 1942 and

educated in Paris. After he earned his doctorate, he took teaching jobs in France and the Congo Republic, but within a few years he was offered a job at the National University of Benin in Cotonou, where he still teaches today.

Much of Hountondji's works center on the nature of African philosophy. One of his books was placed on a list of Africa's 100 best books of the 20th century. That book was *Sur la "philosophie africaine,"* which was originally published in 1976. An English translation was published in 1983 under the title *African Philosophy: Myth and Reality.*

The talent of the Beninois has always been evident in their traditional arts such as music and weaving. But now, in the 21st century, they are beginning to be appreciated for their writing, their philosophy, and their acting skills. In the future perhaps we will see more Beninois names on lists of famous novelists, philosophers, actors, directors, and playwrights.

Readers keenly browse through the collection of books on sale at this roadside bookshop.

LEISURE

MOST PEOPLE in Benin are very poor and do not have the time or resources to spend on leisure activities as people in more developed countries do. Instead of going to movies or playing video games, they listen to the radio or go to friends' houses for a chat. They play traditional games such as *oware* or checkers as well as newer games such as soccer. Children do not often have much time outside their schoolwork and chores, but they will still have some time to play and will often use toys they have made themselves from items they have found. And people of all ages always enjoy the arrival of a traveling theater troupe or a storyteller.

THE MARKET

In Benin many people travel to markets to find what they need. At a market, one can find nearly anything: pots, pans, shoes, spices, crocodile skins, monkey skulls, even chicken feet! Many of the sellers in the market offer items for use in home devotions to the gods of vodun or orisha, while others sell household items. Especially useful are sandals made from old tires. The rubber from the tires is too thick for thorns to puncture, so the farmers who wear the sandals will not have their feet pierced while working in the fields.

Women who sell goods in the market may walk many miles before dawn to be able to set up their stalls. They carry their goods on their heads, and any small children they have who cannot be left at home will be strapped to their backs.

Clothing is rarely sold at the market, but cloth is readily available. Most people buy cloth and then make their own clothes or hire a seamstress

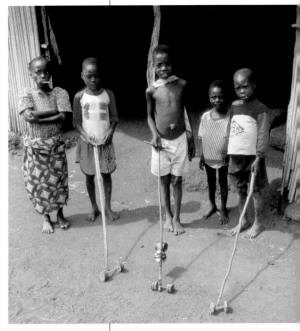

Above: **Most children in Benin play with toys that they make themselves.**

Opposite: **Despite the fact that most Beninois are poor, they enjoy simple leisure activities and the children find inexpensive ways to amuse themselves, such as this boy who is playing hide-and-seek with his friends.**

Household items such as woven baskets and bowls made from dried fruit husks can be found in the markets.

or a tailor to make the clothes. The cloth and the services of the tailor will probably cost less than the equivalent of $20 altogether.

THEATER

People enjoy the antics of traveling theater troupes. When the troupe visits a village, the performers, as all visitors are expected to do, visit the chief's house for his blessing. Once that is secured, the troupe will go to an open area near the village center or market and hang the curtains that divide the stage from the backstage areas. If they have modern equipment such as microphones or lights, the performers will also set those up.

Meanwhile, a *griot*, or traditional storyteller, travels around the village, playing on his drums. People know that means a theatrical performance is imminent. In the next hour or so, people will arrive at the village center, looking for the area where the troupe has set up the equipment.

BOYS AND GIRLS

Children get up at dawn with their families and do their chores. Girls usually have many more chores than boys. Girls are responsible for sweeping the floor, helping with the laundry, taking care of younger siblings, and fetching water, as well as going to school, assuming their families want them to be in school. Boys are responsible for their schoolwork but otherwise often get to play soccer or other games with their friends.

Children often make their own toys out of items they find, such as old tin cans, pieces of wood, or string. Sharing toys is an important part of growing up. A child may have a ball, a doll, or a hoop and a stick with which to roll it. Otherwise they have very little that American children would recognize as toys.

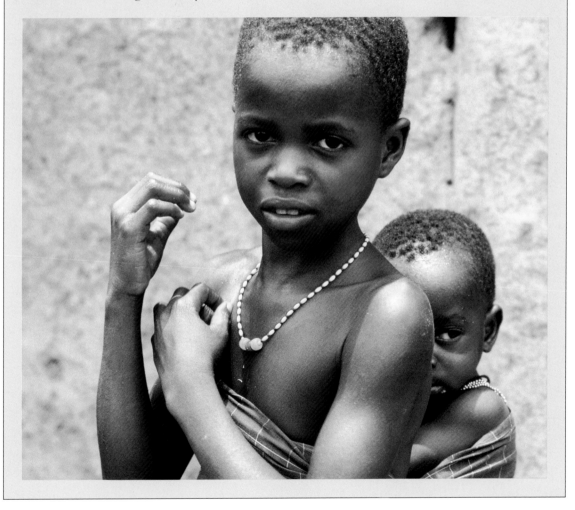

Beninois children enjoy the entertainment and fun that traveling theater troupes and *griots* bring to the village.

When the play is to start, the *griot* begins setting the scene by spinning the tale. Eventually the actors take over and perform the rest of the play.

Most small villages do have radios but do not have access to television and movies, and most people cannot read. Therefore a traveling troupe coming into the village to perform a play will be very popular, and everyone who can attend will.

GRIOTS

Griots can be found across West Africa. They are professional entertainers who keep the oral history and genealogy of their region alive. Traditionally many ceremonies and rituals require the attendance of a *griot* to provide the music. Before a wedding, a *griot* will come to sing to the bride about her new life and reassure her that if her marriage is terrible, she can come home.

One popular traveling theater troupe is called Troupe Bio Guerra.

Because their training is oral, a *griot* must spend many years as an apprentice to a professional. This teacher is usually a father or an uncle. In this way, the oral traditions and songs of a region are passed down through the generations. *Griots* are paid by those who hire them, but the payment is not set, and a *griot* will never exactly know what he might receive as payment. Perhaps it will be cash, or a blanket, or food.

Good *griots* have fantastic memories and can recall long genealogies or vast quantities of local history at a moment's notice. Sometimes a *griot* will have memorized the genealogies of everyone in a village going back 100 or 200 years. Because they can sing someone's praises or ridicule them in song, *griots* are both respected and feared.

In Benin, where access to media is limited, people enjoy gathering for storytelling sessions conducted by *griots*.

Griots must also be adept at playing drums and, in some areas, a 21-stringed instrument called the *kora*, and they must be talented singers. *Griots* are usually men, but sometimes there are female *griots* as well. However, female *griots* (*griottes*) do not travel as widely as their male counterparts, since they are usually tied to their home and the domestic duties of being a wife and mother. *Griottes* sing a special kind of song called a *saabi*, which is considered subversive because it challenges male authority.

In the past, *griots* were often the teachers of royal children, the ones who instructed them on their own family history and the traditions and

Griots, well-versed in the history of their regions, perpetuate the tradition of oral history, as well as help foster a sense of community.

laws of their land. When the chief wished to speak to his village, he whispered to the *griot*, who then repeated the words loudly enough for everyone to hear. Though *griots* do not have royal duties anymore, they remain an integral part of their communities.

For people in Benin, simply surviving is a difficult job. Many of them get by in life by growing crops and bartering their handiwork and excess vegetables for the other things they need. However, people still need to have fun. The Beninois enjoy stories and games just like anyone else, and children can usually find a little time for play in between school and their chores at home.

For many Beninois, life is hard work, but relatively peaceful and not without its little pleasures.

FESTIVALS

MANY OF THE FESTIVALS of Benin revolve around religious observances such as *egungun* festivals, which honor the ancestors, and *gelede* festivals, which offer thanks for the previous harvest and ask that enough rain fall in the new year to grow a new and bountiful harvest. These observances are often done using masquerades.

Masquerades are festivals where some people wear costumes to represent something else: an animal, or an ancestor, or a spirit. The entire costume, not just the headpiece, is referred to as a mask. The goal of the dancer inside the mask is to convey the wishes of the spirit represented by the costume. This can best be done if the identity of the dancer is unknown. To this end, the dancer often uses a disguised voice when speaking as the spirit. People respect and fear the masks because they are the physical manifestations of the spirits they normally pray to and can bring them good luck, a good harvest, and good fortune, or famine, disease, and death.

Above: **Dressed in ritual costumes, these worshipers perform a ceremonial dance at a voodoo festival in Ouidah.**

Opposite: **Festivals in Benin are colorful and vibrant. Here, a woman is dressed in fine attire to participate in a festival.**

Becoming a dancer in a mask is a long and difficult process. Many of the dances that represent the spirits have complicated steps and involve spinning, running, or dancing in difficult rhythms while wearing heavy costumes that are often topped by heavy headgear. Dancers train for years so that they can perform the rituals and dances without disappointing the spirit they represent or the people who look to that spirit for guidance.

EGUNGUN

In orisha, *egungun* is the word for the spirits of the ancestors as a whole. This aspect of the religion assures the dead a place among the living and gives them the responsibility for exhorting the living to uphold traditional standards and ethical mores of past generations. *Egungun* can provide protection or guidance for the living and can even have the power to punish those who have forgotten about their ancestors. To reveal their messages to the living, the *egungun* manifest themselves as masked spirits.

Only those ancestors who are remembered can affect the lives of their descendants. Ancestors who have been forgotten pass on into the realm of the Zamani, where they live with other spirits and gods. Before then, they are in a period called *sasa*, which is the time between the death of their physical body and the death of their memory among the living. When not physically manifested as a masked spirit, ancestors can be invoked at the site of their graves (*oju orori*), at the family shrine (*ile run*), or in the community grave (*igbale*).

These masked dancers represent resurrected ancestors who are respected and feared by their worshipers.

Egungun

The mask of the *egungun* dancer must cover the entire body so that not even the smallest part of the dancer can be seen. The costume is made of raffia in some areas, cloth in others. The headdress of the mask is carved from wood or other material, or can be composed of objects such as skulls, antlers, and even gas masks. Besides remaining hidden inside the costume, the dancer must disguise his voice as he represents the will of the *egungun* speaking through him.

The *egungun* can represent either a specific ancestor who has died, all ancestors of a particular family, or even represent all ancestors corporately. *Egungun* are certain to appear at the annual *egungun* festival, the date of which is set by a diviner. The festival can last 7, 14, 17, or 21 days. During this time, people believe that the ancestors return to them to spend some time among their living descendants. Families negotiate for the days when the mask representing their lineage appears, and on the appointed day, drummers and women of the family sing outside the family compound early in the day. Eventually, the *egungun* arrives, stopping first at the graves of the male members of the family, then visiting the homes of family members. The *egungun* blesses the family and receive their gifts of gratitude. After this, the *egungun* dances through the entire town.

When an *egungun* dispenses advice, the person is bound to follow through with it. Even though the mask is worn by a living person, it is the dead who is speaking and must be obeyed. It is forbidden for anyone

These dancers wear masks made of wood and colorful costumes of cloth and raffia.

115

other than the dancer to touch a mask, and some *egungun* will chase children, who are terrified to be touched, believing that if the *egungun* touches them, they will die. Even adults may be so fearful of the *egungun* that a person who is touched by one might faint or collapse. People who have been touched, or even knocked down by a *egungun*, believe they have offended the *egungun* and will attempt to placate the *egungun* with a gift of cash.

On the days when no adult masks are to appear, the *eegun omokekeke* come out to dance. These are small masks representing children who have died, and the dancers inside are young men who are learning their skills of dancing as a masked dancer. These dances are usually attended by women.

GAANI FESTIVAL

Every year the Bariba celebrate the Gaani festival. This festival celebrates joy, good memories, ethnic solidarity, and Bariba society. An entire month is devoted to finding the funds for the festival. The funds come from villages in the form of money, animals, food, and clothing. Babies, both male and female, born during this month are given the name Gaani before their first name.

When the festival is only a week away, the king invites powerful sorcerers to his palace so that they may cast spells which will protect the celebration and everyone involved. The night before the festival, drums and trumpets are brought out and played all night long.

Vodun worshipers attend festivals with charms and ritual objects attached to their clothes.

EGUN BLA

Some masks represent certain spirits. One of these is Egun Bla, which is one of the most feared spirits of the *egungun*. Egun Bla symbolizes the dark side of Yoruba religious beliefs. The spirit is offered sacrifices and gifts to appease its vengeful nature. Egun Bla is so powerful that it is believed that hearing it speak would drive a person mad. People do not only fear Egun Bla, however, but they also appeal to it for assistance. A woman who wants to have a child may ask to make a sacrifice before the spirit so that her wish will come true.

In the morning on the day of the festival, there is a horse show. In the afternoon, the king and his court emerge from his palace to the music of drums and trumpets and the cheering of the people. They will walk for miles to visit sites sacred to the Bariba.

This procession consists of the king and his court followed by musicians. After the musicians come other dignitaries such as the man in charge of the ceremonies and the king's chief poet and genealogist. Behind them come horsemen, and the crowd follows at the end. All told, this procession will travel just over seven miles (12 km) and visit nine sites.

The sacred sites to be visited include Too Yankou Bakararou, where the king says his prayers; Dakirou, where the graves of legendary heroes Bake Doue and his brother Sero Betete are located; and Bankpilou, where the tomb of King Kpe Gounou Kaba Wouko is located.

Once the procession is completed, the king returns to his palace, where he receives the well-wishes of his subjects for another happy and prosperous year.

GELEDE FESTIVAL

The Yoruba Gelede festival occurs between March and May every year. At this festival, members of the *gelede* society dance to express gratitude for the previous harvest and to invoke the rains for the next plantings. The dance honors the ancestral mother of the Yoruba, Iya Nla, who embodies the order inherent in society but who also encompasses a chaotic side. The festival aims to appease or eliminate the negative aspects of Iya Nla and to encourage the beneficial side of her nature.

The masked dancers of the *gelede* festival dance in time to the beating of drums. The drumbeats come faster and faster until the dancer is a whirling blur. However, the headdress of the costume remains still. This is to embody the Yoruba ideal of summoning peace in a chaotic world. *Gelede* dancers begin their training when they are five years old.

ZANGBETO MASQUERADE

During the dry season, the Fon hold their Zangbeto masquerade. This ceremony is to honor the spirits and is believed to renew the spirituality of the community and the land. This will ensure prosperity and fertility throughout the area. The name of the ceremony comes from the words

A Zangbeto mask followed by worshipers from the village. Each mask has a guardian to lead the way for the dancer.

zan ("night") and *beto* ("person"). It is also known as The Coming Out of the Spirits. The spirits honored were traditionally the ones that protected the kings, the chiefs, and the elders. The Zangbeto masked dancers also act as enforcers of a ruler's authority. They may behave like policemen, maintaining the security of the village at night against bandits. Because people are afraid to be confronted by the masked dancers, they stay in their homes during the night. The dancers sing songs of warning as they enter a village at dusk to remind people to return to their homes. Those who do not obey risk punishment for violating this sacred curfew.

The masks are composed of a raffia costume with a headress on top, giving them a height of nine feet or more. Because of the confining nature of the costume, each masked dancer has a guardian who helps guide him through the village. The dancing rids the village of all evil forces, protecting it until the next dry season, when the masked dancers will emerge from the bush singing their songs and dancing energetically once again.

The Beninois have developed elaborate rituals to help them through the important milestones in their lives such as birth, marriage, childbirth,

Dancers in preparation for the annual Zangbeto festival. They wear colorful and tall masks as they make their way through the village, protecting and blessing the community.

and death. Even after death, ancestors continue to visit families in the form of masks and exert influence over the families from the other side. People respect the masks and fear them. Rituals such as marriage and the mask dances bring people together and reinforce their place in the community.

VODUN DAY

Since 1992, Vodun Day has been celebrated in Benin on January 10. As a religion, vodun was suppressed during colonial times, and then continued

Vodun Day is celebrated throughout Benin. Here, a group of worshipers perform a ceremonial dance at Ouidah.

to be repressed under Matthieu Kerekou's regime. However, by 1990, the religion was once again openly practiced and since 1992 it has been recognized as one of the country's official religions.

Former president of Benin, Nicephore Soglo, claimed vodun spirits saved his life and in gratitude, he established Vodun Day. When Mattieu Kerekou regained power, he attempted to abolish the holiday, but was unsuccessful. Kerekou himself is the son of a vodun priestess.

Many of the main festivities occur in Ouidah, where slaves were loaded onto ships at a beach called "the point of no return." Today, people gather on that same beach to play music, dance, pray, and sacrifice animals to the spirits. Other people listen to speeches which praise the religion's positive influence on people's lives. Many people feel the day is not only a festival to remember vodun but also to remember the untold thousands of Beninois who were taken away in slavery over the centuries.

Although most attendees in Ouidah are from Benin, many people on the beach have traveled from the United States, Brazil, and Haiti. These people have come to discover something about the culture of their ancestors who were slaves.

Beninois from the north bring horses and, for part of the day, the beach becomes an impromptu racetrack and a place to display one's riding skills. At the end of the day, priests often have feasts at their homes and invite many people to join them, including people who have traveled from other countries to learn about Vodun Day and the religion of their ancestors.

During Vodun Day in 2005, priests sacrificed chickens and goats to the spirits and prayed for the victims of the Asian tsunami disaster which occurred on December 26, 2004. Over 150,000 people died across 11 countries in that tsunami. Priests asked the spirits to "relieve the pain" of those who had been affected by the disaster.

FOOD

BENIN has a wealth of variations of food traditions among its ethnic groups, but the main divisions are between north and south. Even so, every village will have a slightly different style, so trying food everywhere you go will always be a new and exciting, as well as tasty, experience.

EVERYDAY FOODS

In the south, corn is the main staple of everyone's diet. Corn flour is used to make dough, which is cooked and served with sauces made from peanuts or tomatoes. The meats most often eaten are fish and chicken, which are usually fried. Palm or peanut oil is used in the frying. Less commonly, people eat goat, rabbit, and even bush rat. Rice, couscous, and beans are eaten quite commonly. In the south, it is usually easy to get fresh fruits such as oranges, bananas, pineapples, and mangoes.

Above: **These women prepare corn for cooking. Corn is a staple in the south of Benin.**

Opposite: **Markets are a colorful sight in Benin, with a large variety of local produce for sale.**

In the north, yams are much more common than corn. Yams are pounded into a flour, cooked, and eaten with sauces. Pounding the yams into the flour is time-consuming, and sometimes several women will cooperate in the task, taking turns. During the day, one can hear the thunking sound of the women of the village pounding the yam flesh into flour.

As in the south, the sauces that are eaten with the corn or yam dough are often based on tomatoes or peanuts. For meat, people most commonly eat beef, pork, and chicken. As the north is not near the ocean, and long-distance travel is not easy, fish is not as common once you leave the coastal areas. Many northern people make cheese. They also eat rice, couscous, and beans, just as people do in the south. Fruits are abundant during certain seasons, especially mangoes.

YAMS

The yams eaten in Benin are real yams, not the sweet potatoes of American grocery stores, which are sometimes referred to as yams.

Sweet potatoes (*Ipomoea batatas*) belong to the morning-glory family and are native to the tropics of the Americas. Columbus brought them to Europe. They are orange or yellow tubers that taper to a point.

Yams (*Dioscorea batatas*), on the other hand, are not even distantly related to potatoes or sweet potatoes. They were originally cultivated in West Africa around 8000 B.C. The tuber has a dark brown or black skin, which covers off-white, purple, or red flesh inside, depending on the variety. The word *yam* also comes from west Africa; in several languages the verb "to eat" can be pronounced *njam*, *nyami*, or *djambi*.

Yams can grow to be seven feet long and can weigh 120 pounds (50 kg)! Yams must be cooked to remove a substance called dioscorene, which tastes bitter and is mildly toxic to humans.

People eat their meals with their fingers. Much of the meal is in the form of a doughy ball that they dip in sauce. The ball is made from rice, millet, sorghum, or corn, which is boiled and stirred until it is stiff enough to form into balls. Meat is served in cubes, as are cheese, fish, and eggs. This way everything can easily be eaten with the fingers.

At the markets, women try to sell local delicacies such as bush rat and slugs cooked with onions and hot peppers. Many times these women station themselves near the places where taxis stop and will wave food under the noses of people just getting out of the taxis to tempt them to try their cooking.

When buying food at the market, the customer does not tell the seller how much food he or she wants but rather how much money he or she will spend. The woman selling the food then doles out however much rice or corn balls would make up that cost and dumps them in some sauce. Bowls and plates are not disposable; once you use them, you must return them so that the women can clean them and have them ready for the next customer.

Women selling fried dough pastries is a common sight in Benin.

In Benin people eat nearly every part of an animal, including fish heads, goat heads, and intestines. This helps the food go further and feed more people.

125

Large varieties of fruits and vegetables are sold in the markets.

A food often served for breakfast is *koko*, a kind of hot cereal that is strained and eaten with a spoon. If one buys *koko* at the market, it may be served in a plastic bag. The customer bites a hole in the bag and drinks the *koko*. At night, it is more common to see a hot cereal made from cassava, like tapioca. Roasted peanuts or sugar is often added to this dish.

Some people in Benin make a cheese called *wagasi*. It is made by placing milk into a bowl with a tree sap that helps the milk congeal. This mixture is left out until it turns into cheese. The *wagasi* is then cut up into cubes and fried before eating.

The cheapest food, which is eaten by the very poor, is made out of *gari*. *Gari* is cassava flour. People add water to it and drink the mixture cold. People who have run out of food before the harvest and have no money eat *gari* until the harvest comes in.

Local breweries in Benin make their own varieties of beer, including La Beninoise, Flag, and Castel. *Tchoucoutou* is a very thick, sweet beer brewed in the north, especially around Parakou. Another alcoholic drink made in Benin is *sodabi*, which is distilled from palm wine. People like to have *sodabi* at parties and celebrations such as weddings.

TABLE MANNERS

People in Benin always wash their hands before eating, even if washing consists of merely rinsing off their hands in some water. People eat only with their right hands; to eat with the left hand is considered very rude.

Bread is often sold on the streets. This bread seller's "hat" not only shields her from the sun but can also be used as a plate.

127

Talking while eating is also considered rude. Children are warned to be quiet or else they might choke. They are also taught not to reach for food, that an adult will get it for them. Children often get to eat whatever is left when the adults are finished.

If people walk by, it is considered polite to invite them to eat with you, because it is impolite to simply eat in front of others. If you are sharing a taxi, do not be surprised if you are offered part of someone else's snack! In these circumstances, it is polite to say thank you but to refuse to take any.

Everyone in the family eats out of the same bowl. Often the men eat separately from the women and the children. In families that follow more Western customs, men, women, and children may all eat together.

For celebrations like Eid or Easter or Christmas, families will prepare a great deal of food to offer to anyone who comes by. Because people

Children at this Ouissi village enjoy fermented cassava wrapped in leaves for lunch.

A family watches over bowls of fermented cassava, which is a staple food for many.

do not have phones, they keep in touch with their families and friends by dressing in their best and then stopping by for a visit on holidays. Visitors are always offered something to eat, even if they are beggars going around the village. For these special occasions, women will prepare salads and bread, which they will rarely serve at any other time.

The people of Benin cook a wide variety of foods, though the main forms are dough balls dipped in sauce and various types of hot cereals. Women prepare excellent meals using ingredients they buy at the market or grow at home. Hospitality is always taken very seriously, and anyone who comes by will be offered something to eat. The hospitality and good cooking make Benin a wonderful place to try many types of delicious foods.

LEGUME SAUCE

½ onion
1 teaspoons pimento
Garlic
1 small tomato (or 2 tablespoons tomato paste)
2 tablespoons oil
2 cups water
1 bullion cube
Fish sauce
1½ cups collard greens
½ cup of kidney beans, boiled and drained

Saute the onion, pimento, garlic, and tomato paste in oil for a few minutes. Add water, bullion cube, and fish sauce. Simmer for 15 minutes. Add collard greens and kidney beans. Cook for 5 more minutes.

KLUI KLUI

1 pound unsalted peanuts

Place unsalted peanuts in blender, and blend until you get peanut butter. Let sit for a day so the the oil separates from the solids. Drain oil off to use for frying. Shape peanut solids into sticks and fry in the oil.

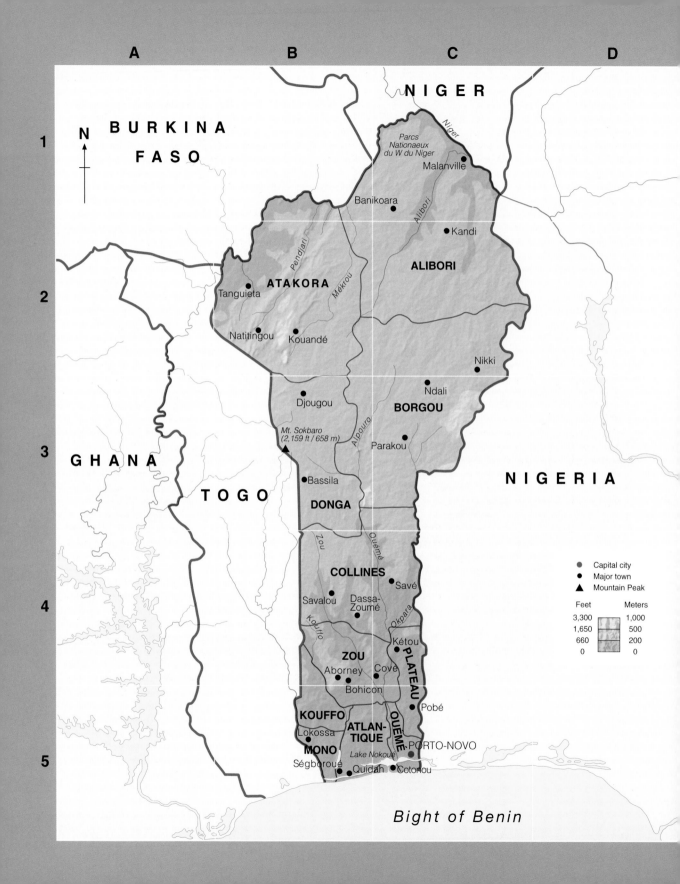

MAP OF BENIN

ECONOMIC BENIN

Agriculture

- Cassava and peanuts
- Corn
- Cotton
- Palm Fruit
- Yams

Services

- Hydroelectricity
- Tourism

Natural Resources

- Fish
- Gold
- Iron
- Phosphates

ABOUT THE ECONOMY

OVERVIEW
During the Beninois Revolution, the government turned to a socialist style of economy. By 1990 the economy was in ruins and the government instituted a free-market economy in its place. Since then, the economy has grown steadily at roughly 5 percent per year, though it is still underdeveloped and remains dependent on subsistence agriculture. An increase in population has offset much of the gains made by economic growth.

GROSS DOMESTIC PRODUCT (GDP)
$8.338 billion (2004 estimate)

GDP BY SECTOR
Agriculture 36.3 percent, industry 14.3 percent, services 49.4 percent (2004 estimate)

POPULATION BELOW POVERTY LINE
37 percent (2001 estimate)

INFLATION RATE
2.8 percent (2004 estimate)

CURRENCY
Central African franc (XOF)
US$1 = $556.58 XOF (December 2005)
Coins: $1, $5, $10, $25, $50, $100, $250
Notes: $500, $1,000, $2,000, $5,000, $10,000

AGRICULTURAL PRODUCTS
Cassava, corn, cotton, yams, beans, peanuts, palm oil, fish

INDUSTRIAL PRODUCTS
Textiles, food processing, construction materials

MAJOR EXPORTS
Cotton, crude oil, palm products, cocoa

MAJOR IMPORTS
Food, petroleum products

TOURISM
145,000 tourists per year

MAJOR TRADE PARTNERS
China, France, India, Thailand

CULTURAL BENIN

National Parc du W du Niger
The most remote national park in Benin, where one can see aardvarks, cheetahs, and many kinds of birds.

National Parc de Pendjari
A wildlife park where a wide variety of animals, including lions and elephants, can be found.

Mount Sokbaro
The highest point in the country.

Abomey
Historically the capital of the kingdom of Dohomey. Today it is home to an impressive museum and many craft workers.

Allada
The capital of the kingdom of Ardra, which thrived from the 16th to the 17th century.

Ouidah
The port where slaves left the country. The Gate of No Return, through which slaves walked on their way to be loaded onto ships, is in Ouidah.

ABOUT THE CULTURE

COUNTRY NAME
Republic of Benin

CAPITAL
Porto Novo is the official capital, but the seat of government is in Cotonou

NATIONAL ANTHEM
"L'Aube Novelle" ("A New Dawn")

OTHER MAJOR CITIES
Ouidah, Parakou, Djougou, Abomey

STATE FLAG
Two equal horizontal bands of yellow (on top) and red, with a vertical green band on the hoist side

POPULATION
7,250,000

ETHNIC GROUPS
Fon, Adja, Yoruba, Bariba

LIFE EXPECTANCY
50.81 years

RELIGIONS
Native religions 50 percent, Christianity 30 percent, Islam 20 percent

OFFICIAL LANGUAGE
French

LITERACY RATE
40.9 percent

NATIONAL HOLIDAYS
January 10 (Vondun Day)
August 1 (Independence Day)

TIME LINE

IN BENIN	IN THE WORLD
	753 B.C. Rome is founded.
	A.D. 600 Height of Mayan civilization
	1530 Beginning of trans-Atlantic slave trade organized by the Portuguese in Africa.
1620 The Kingdom of Dahomey is founded.	**1620** Pilgrims sail the Mayflower to America.
1730 Dahomey becomes a tributary state of the Yoruba kingdom of Oyo.	**1776** U.S. Declaration of Independence
1818 Dahomey shakes off Oyo overlordship under King Ghézo.	**1789–99** The French Revolution **1869** The Suez Canal is opened.
1892–94 War with the French	
1894 King Béhanzin is deposed, Amazon warriors are massacred, and France installs a puppet king.	**1914** World War I begins. **1939** World War II begins. **1945** The United States drops atomic bombs on Hiroshima and Nagasaki.
1960 Dahomey becomes independent of France.	
1963 First major government collapse.	
1965 The government collapses; Christophe Soglo is installed in power.	
1967 Soglo is replaced by Maurice Kouandete.	

IN BENIN	IN THE WORLD
1968 A new government is established by Emile Zinsou.	
1972 Mathieu Kerekou begins his socialist policies.	
1975 Kerekou's regime changes the name of the country from Dahomey to People's Republic of Benin.	
1985 Student demonstrations against Kerekou's regime are put down by force.	
	1986 Nuclear power disaster at Chernobyl in Ukraine
1990 A new constitution is ratified, and the country becomes a democracy.	
1991 Nicephore Soglo is elected president.	**1991** Break-up of the Soviet Union
1992 Benin legalizes Vodun Day as a national holiday, to take place every January 10.	
1996 Kerekou is elected president.	**1997** Hong Kong is returned to China.
1999 The country's six provinces are divided into 12 departments.	
2001 Kerekou is reelected president.	**2001** Terrorists crash planes in New York, Washington, D.C., and Pennsylvania.
2003 National Assembly elections are held.	**2003** War in Iraq
2005 The G8 agree to eliminate much of Benin's foreign debt.	
2006 Yayi Boni is elected president.	

GLOSSARY

Adja
An ethnic group, related to the Fon, living in the southern part of Benin.

ahosi
Wives of the king of Dahomey.

ahovi
Royal children of the king of Dahomey.

aso oke
Traditional Yoruba cloths made by men, including *etu*, *sanyan*, and *alaari*.

aze
Bad magic that harms people.

babalao
A Yoruba diviner.

bata
A Yoruba drum ensemble.

bo
Good magic that aids people.

bokono
A Fon diviner.

"Brazilians"
The educated elite of French-ruled Dahomey, descendants of slaves who had returned to Africa.

daklo
A woman who took a petitioner's words to the king of Dahomey and returned with his answer.

egungun
Yoruba term for the spirits of the ancestors as a whole.

fa
In vodun, a person's destiny.

griot
A traditional storyteller and historian, a keeper of oral traditions.

houngan
A male vodun priest.

hovi
Statues that represent twins among the Fon.

kijipa
A traditional indigo-and-white striped Yoruba cloth woven by women.

kpojito
The reign-mate of the king of Dahomey, a woman always chosen from the common people.

manbo
A female vodun priest.

ori
In orisha, a person's destiny.

orisha
The native religion of the Yoruba.

sodabi
A strong alcoholic drink made from palm fruit.

FURTHER INFORMATION

BOOKS

Koslow, Philip. *Dahomey: The Warrior Kings*. Philadelphia: Chelsea House Publishers, 1996.
Mama, Raouf. *Why Goats Smell Bad and Other Stories from Benin*. North Haven, CT: Linnet Books, 1998.
Van Gelder, Alex, and Okwui Enwezor. *Life and Afterlife in Benin*. Boston: Phaidon Press, 2005.

WEBSITES

Africaguide.com. www.africaguide.com/features/trvafmag/036.htm.
Africanhiphop.com.
    www.africanhiphop.com/modules.php?file=article&name=News&op=modload&sid=38.
Central Intelligence Agency World Factbook. (Select Benin from the country list)
    www.cia.gov/cia/publications/factbook/index.html
Fon Is Fun. www.geocities.com/fon_is_fun/
Human Rights Watch: Benin. http://hrw.org/doc/?t=africa&c=benin
Lonely Planet World Guide: Destination Benin.
    www.lonelyplanet.com/worldguide/destinations/africa/benin
Wikipedia. http://en.wikipedia.org/wiki/Benin

VIDEOS

Discovering Benin, West Africa. Chris Starace, 2004.
West Africa Benin, Mali, Burkina Faso. Lonely Planet, 1997.

MUSIC

Lacerda, Marcos Branda. *The World's Musical Traditions 8: Yoruba Drums from Benin, West Africa*. Smithsonian Folkways Recordings, 1996.

BIBLIOGRAPHY

Alpern, Stanley B. *Amazons of Black Sparta: The Women Warriors of Dahomey.* New York: New York University Press, 1998.

Bay, Edna G. *Wives of the Leopard: Gender, Politics, and Culture in the Kingdom of Dahomey.* Charlottesville, VA: University of Virginia Press, 1998.

Beckwith, Carol, and Angela Fisher. *African Ceremonies*, Vols 1 & 2. New York: Harry N. Abrams, 1999.

Blier, Suzanne Preston. *African Vodun: Art, Psychology, and Power.* Chicago: University of Chicago Press, 1995.

Campbell, W. Joseph. *The Emergent Independent Press in Benin and Cote d'Ivoire.* Westport, CT: Praeger, 1998.

Clarke, Duncan. *The Art of African Textiles.* San Diego: Thunder Bay Press, 1997.

DeCarlo, Samuel. *Historical Dictionary of Benin, Third Edition.* Lanham, MD: The Scarecrow Press, 1997.

Olupona, Jacob K. (editor). *African Spirituality: Forms, Meanings, and Expressions.* New York: The Crossroad Publishing Co., 2000.

Sargent, Carolyn Fishel. *Maternity, Medicine, and Power: Reproductive Decisions in Urban Benin.* Berkeley: University of California Press, 1989.

Atti-Mama, Cyriaque. "Co-Management in Continental Fishing in Benin: The Case of Lake Nokoue." Proceedings of the International Workshop on Fisheries Co-Management. www.worldfishcenter.org/Pubs/Way%20Forward/12%20Atti-Mama.pdf.

Benin Government Portal. www.gouv.bj/en/index.php.

Benintourisme.com. www.benintourisme.com

CIA.gov. www.odci.gov/cia/publications/factbook/geos/bn.html.

CNN.com. www.cnn.com/2005/WORLD/africa/04/30/togo/index.html.

Encyclopedia.com. www.encyclopedia.com/html/section/beninaf_history.asp.

Ethnologue.com. www.ethnologue.com/show_country.asp?name=Benin.

Exxun.com. www.exxun.com/Benin/d_gv.html.

Mamiwata.com. www.mamiwata.com/Benin.html.

Opentopia.com. http://encycl.opentopia.com/term/Gbe_languages.

Religioustolerance.org. www.religioustolerance.org/voodoo.htm.

US-Africa.tripod.com. http://us-africa.tripod.com/benin.html.

Chris Starace. *Discovering Benin, West Africa.* 2004. (DVD)

Lacerda, Marcos Branda. *The World's Musical Traditions 8: Yoruba Drums from Benin, West Africa.* Smithsonian Folkways Recordings, 1996.

INDEX